PLOUGHSHARES

Spring 1995 · Vol. 21, No. 1

GUEST EDITOR
Gary Soto

EXECUTIVE DIRECTOR
DeWitt Henry

EDITOR
Don Lee

POETRY EDITOR
David Daniel

ASSOCIATE EDITOR
Jessica Dineen

EDITORIAL ASSISTANT
Jodee Stanley

FOUNDING PUBLISHER
Peter O'Malley

ADVISORY EDITORS

Russell Banks
Anne Bernays
Frank Bidart
Rosellen Brown
James Carroll
Madeline DeFrees
Rita Dove
Andre Dubus
Carolyn Forché
George Garrett
Lorrie Goldensohn
David Gullette
Marilyn Hacker
Donald Hall
Paul Hannigan
Stratis Haviaras
Fanny Howe

Marie Howe
Justin Kaplan
Bill Knott
Maxine Kumin
Philip Levine
Thomas Lux
Gail Mazur
James Alan McPherson
Leonard Michaels
Sue Miller
Jay Neugeboren
Tim O'Brien
Joyce Peseroff
Jayne Anne Phillips
Robert Pinsky
James Randall
Alberto Alvaro Ríos

M. L. Rosenthal
Lloyd Schwartz
Jane Shore
Charles Simic
Maura Stanton
Gerald Stern
Christopher Tilghman
Richard Tillinghast
Chase Twichell
Fred Viebahn
Ellen Bryant Voigt
Dan Wakefield
Derek Walcott
James Welch
Alan Williamson
Tobias Wolff
Al Young

PLOUGHSHARES, a journal of new writing, is guest-edited serially by prominent writers who explore different and personal visions, aesthetics, and literary circles. PLOUGHSHARES is published in April, August, and December at Emerson College, 100 Beacon Street, Boston, MA 02116-1596. Telephone: (617) 578-8753.

EDITORIAL INTERNS: Michelle Heller and Robin Troy. POETRY READERS: Rebecca Lavine, Mary-Margaret Mulligan, Leslie Haynes, Tom Laughlin, Renee Rooks, Lisa Sewell, Karen Voelker, Tanja Brull, Brijit Brown, and Bethany Daniel. FICTION READERS: Billie Lydia Porter, Karen Wise, Joseph Connolly, Maryanne O'Hara, Michael Rainho, Kevin Supples, Barbara Lewis, David Watta, Kimberley Reynolds, David Rowell, Elizabeth Rourke, Will Morton, and Loretta Chen.

SUBSCRIPTIONS (ISSN 0048-4474): $19/domestic and $24/international for individuals; $22/domestic and $27/international for institutions. See last page for order form.

UPCOMING: Fall 1995, a fiction issue edited by Ann Beattie, will appear in August 1995. Winter 1995-96, a fiction and poetry issue edited by Tim O'Brien and Mark Strand, will appear in December 1995. Spring 1996, a poetry and fiction issue edited by Marilyn Hacker, will appear in April 1996.

SUBMISSIONS: Please see page 211 for detailed submission policies.

Classroom-adoption and back-issue orders may be placed directly through *Ploughshares*. Authorization to photocopy journal pieces may be obtained by contacting *Ploughshares* for permission and paying a fee of 5¢ per page, per copy. Microfilms of back issues may be obtained from University Microfilms. *Ploughshares* is also available as CD-ROM and full-text products from EBSCO, H.W. Wilson, Information Access, and University Microfilms.

Indexed in M.L.A. Bibliography, American Humanities Index, Index of American Periodical Verse, Book Review Index. Self-index through Volume 6 available from the publisher; annual supplements appear in the fourth number of each subsequent volume. The views and opinions expressed in this journal are solely those of the authors. All rights for individual works revert to the authors upon publication.

Distributed by Bernhard DeBoer (113 E. Centre St., Nutley, NJ 07110), Fine Print Distributors (500 Pampa Dr., Austin, TX 78752), Ingram Periodicals (1226 Heil Quaker Blvd., La Vergne, TN 37086), and L-S Distributors (436 North Canal St. #7, South San Francisco, CA 94080).

Printed in the United States of America on recycled paper by Edwards Brothers.

CONTENTS

Spring 1995

Introduction

When *Ploughshares* first called me about editing this issue, it was a cool afternoon, thanks to an early fog rolling in from the San Francisco Bay, and I was in the garage working out with Gerardo G., a kickboxer and recent graduate in electrical engineering from UC Berkeley. He was pummeling me next to a bunch of cartons which contained remainders of my books. When I heard the cordless telephone ring, I gratefully pulled away from the massacre of my flesh to answer the call. I breathed into the phone, "Yeah, man..." The call was obviously long-distance, because the voice was polite and articulate. Almost everyone who calls me—my brothers, usually, or ruddy-faced writers I know—is impolite and rude. I heard the editor out and was happy not so much about his assignment, but for having a moment to reflect on the temporality of a quickly aging body. I needed rest. I needed three or four new lungs to keep up with my opponent, Gerardo, who is built like G.I. Joe, but many times larger, and who used to be one bad dude when he ran with a gang in Ciudad Juárez, Mexico. As for me, a failed professor with a hairline in massive retreat, I resemble Mrs. Butterworth, that beautiful breakfast helper spanked on a stack of pancakes. In short, I needed that call.

I agreed to put together an issue and left the theme up in the air for several weeks. I went about living and writing and nurturing a small garden of fog-dwarfed beefsteak tomatoes in the backyard. The next time I boxed with Gerardo, he had stern instructions from his girlfriend, a future elementary school teacher, not to hurt me. When asked why, she responded that I was the only Mexican-American children's writer in the country, and I needed to remain intact. Thus, Gerardo was now a piece of cake and, for me, a real confidence builder. I was doing the Mrs. Butterworth two-step shuffle when I got a second call from the editor of *Ploughshares,* asking if I had arrived at a theme for the issue. Caught off-guard, I breathed heavily into the phone something about everyday evil and sexuality, in part because I remembered the two subjects as popular themes in Sunday homilies, and because I had some unfinished business with the Catholic faith.

Between the years 1985 and 1990, I had returned to the church with a vengeance. I won't explain exactly why I was brought to my knees, but I will provide evidence: for three years I went to Mass not once but twice a day; I moved my family to San Francisco so we could be close to the church that I loved, namely Old St. Mary; I considered joining *Opus Dei*, a fundamentalist religious group; I sent my daughter to Catholic school with her hair cut like a novice nun; I joined a young-adult group; I lay on a wooden cross during a weekend retreat; I bought a used set of Catholic encyclopedias that I thought would set me straight (the language, however, was dull and so packed with hocus-pocus theories that I needed NoDoz to keep turning the pages). Thus, those five intense years in the Catholic faith resulted in a new set of friends, prayer, peculiar dreams, one therapist, three overseas adoptions, and two books: *Lesser Evils* and *Home Course in Religion*, both of which are now out of print and whose themes concern lust, faith, childhood, and disease—a hodgepodge of reactions to my Catholic upbringing.

Ploughshares dutifully announced the theme I had proposed, but it ended up baffling editors and writers alike. In fact, *Ploughshares* has since changed its editorial practices—they no longer put together issues with themes in mind—and I have a sneaking suspicion I'm to blame, because no one was certain what the heck I meant by everyday evil and sexuality.

By evil, I was thinking of those moments of wickedness that live inside us and occasionally surface and manifest themselves, not only in thought but also in ugly and deplorable actions. A case in point: I remember sitting with a bunch of guys in Fresno, and everyone was drunk or drugged or both. The coals of the barbecue had died down, along with the conversation. Attention was given over to a little girl, someone's daughter, as she played with a kitten only a few weeks old. A monstrous dog was in the rear of the disheveled yard, chained and barking, disturbing the peaceful quiet of the neighborhood. Against the orange porchlight, I knew these men were wicked beyond description. When the girl disap-

peared into the house, one guy got it into his head to feed the kit-
ten to the dog, which he did. He picked it up without much
thought, as he might a baseball mitt or Frisbee, giggled, staggered
over to the chained dog, and held the kitten over its head until it
was yapping and writhing and frothing. When the guy let the kit-
ten go, the men circled in a ring to watch the dog's manic destruc-
tion. Most everyone laughed when the girl reappeared and asked
about the kitten. I wasn't so drunk that I didn't feel contempt for
these people, if "people" is the right word. I left and drove around
my hometown Fresno, a town where the worse you feel, the worse
you're treated. And I was feeling pretty bad that night, and lay my
head down with a godawful weight.

As for sexuality, I was thinking how, after our attention to
sports, the media proclaims sex as America's most luxurious pas-
time, though, of course, we may see it as a brief grunt and a
whimper in our own households. But the media has our atten-
tion. You would think from its display on the airwaves that in
every dinky town across the country, east to west, north to south,
people were screwing with marvelous and prolific abandon. Sex-
ual messages are pervasive—sometimes subtle, sometimes not,
embodied in sundry vehicles, from the shape of perfume bottles
to thong bikinis, one of the few articles of clothing with which a
person could get the floss of a lifetime. Certainly we writers, I
thought, might have something to say about the play of the media
upon our senses.

I imagined receiving manuscripts with comic stories about sex-
uality—humorous confessions about reckless eyeballing, for
instance, or disturbingly open accounts of adultery. If sexual
appetites don't bring on clouds of confusion and remorse, they
must bring raunchy laughter, as when a *tejano* friend told me
about his first sexual encounter: When he opened his date's bare
legs, he discovered a confetti-like flake of toilet paper stuck to her
bottom. He asked me, rhetorically, if that sight stopped him, a
nineteen-year-old, from yanking off his shitkickers and undoing
his horse-stenciled leather belt. Not a chance. He said to me, "At
least I knew my honey wiped."

In November, I began to get my first batches of manuscripts
from the editors, and the business of selecting began. By then,

with the issue now called "Everyday Seductions," I had abandoned the original themes and was searching for a more sordid and frightening peek at the underside of our broken and seedy world. As we know, happy literature has no history, and if literature is meant to remain, it has a better chance when it revels in a rough and ugly terrain. I was a camel looking for the kind of writing that is not so much sensational as it is honest, brutal, lonely, introspective, and, yes, comical. And while I did solicit from five writers, I intended from the get-go to give space to unsolicited manuscripts, thus allowing an open invitation. Readers will find familiar names, such as fiction writers Dagoberto Gilb and Susan Dodd and poets Kenneth Rosen and Martín Espada. However, there are surprises with every turned page. That will be your delight; mine is that my initial proposition took a curve, and I arrived in a wholly unsuspected place, peopled with writers I didn't know or knew only from a distance. That is the beauty of editing an issue of *Ploughshares,* assembling it for the sake of getting firsthand peeks.

And Gerardo, the Mexican kickboxer? He's in Georgia working on an advanced engineering degree. My gloves hang on a nail in the garage, and my mouthpiece is grinning in a top drawer. On some days, when the sun is out and I'm in my garage shadowboxing, I like to pretend that my threatening presence, my jab and body shot, the swiftness of my feet, ran Gerardo, my brown brother, out of town.

JON VEINBERG

The Jogger

For six months
each day at sunrise
I've watched a woman
in bright red trunks
run past my window
and each time I think
of how as a boy
I took my stance
in front of the steamed
mirror, my faded boxers
safety-pinned proudly
at the crotch
and judged my body
against all things
that might cause it harm.
      And I remember
reading of an eighty-
two-year-old man who
planned to run fifty miles
backwards into the heat
of Nebraska and later
on Late Nite Cable Sports
I watched him wave off
a blur of insects
bedazzled by his face,
the corn stalks swayed,
weeds draped
the storefront awnings
and the telephone poles
passed into a world
of shadows. I saw
men hiccup their toothpicks

and women bury their hands
into their aprons
when he soiled his pants
as he crossed the finish line.
      And I remember
flooding the coffee table
with beer and yelling
into those zoomed-in,
sunstroked eyes that I'll
weigh my towel-patched armchair
and half pint of cheap shit
on his feel-good scale
anytime because I too once
set out to shatter
the world's mark—
my arms swinging
against the clock
like two pinwheels
desiring to grab someone
who'd come along for the ride.
I huffed and puffed
for seven years thinking
it was true love
until someone told me
I can't beat anyone's record
but can be modestly compared
to minimum wage. I
wanted to run across the water
but that'd been done before,
vertically, sideways, 10K's
in somersault fashion
and now, if that woman
who runs past my house
each morning were to lose
her breath at my window,
look in and find me limp
and slouched
among the white noise and cigarettes

charring the carpet
how would she ever know
that I once believed
in a sure road to grace,
that I still believe in miracles?

Motel Drive

Next door
the room is padlocked
from the outside; inside
the children are ransacking
the cupboards and playing
catch with the empty
Cool Whip containers
and most afternoons
you could've found me
behind any one of these blue-
stained doors, my girdles
unhitched, my dusty nylons
flagging the window,
contesting the smoke rings
that peel off these sluggish
lips like clouds being freed
from a sore and blistered earth.
You could've plotted out
any old highway that angled
into the railroad tracks
and found me tucked between,
sleep's week-old spittle
on my cheek, spooning the lumpy
pudding and refusing weight.
You could've tossed your jacket
into the sperm-stained closet
and waited out the weak pulse
of noon, the haggle and choke
of the water cooler, and the sun's
desire to flash against the tin-
foiled courtyard.
        Buttermilk and crosstops
for dinner. The truckers
and three-legged dogs scuffle

beneath the neon's ferocity
and you could've asked for Ginger
or Blossom or Bonnie Blaze
and been steered to me. You
could've tracked the whiff of sour mesh
and sweet sin into the Miracle Inn Club
where men in dark tilted hats
roll the bones for another
round of widowmakers, and heard
through the fractured glow
of the TV how sad it was
for the tall blond daughters
of millionaires to have gone
so easily berserk. You could've
followed me to the chain-link
fence, high heels dangling
from my purse, at the intersection
of cracked ribs and a thousand winks.
You could've slipped past
the tortilla hawkers dodging
the tow trucks, the cats
pairing off in dumpsters,
and the yellow fist of morning
to take my wrist, thin
as a membrane into your hand.
    You could've
stretched out on the rollaway,
felt the pistol's cool nozzle
hidden in the cushions
and watched me will myself
to sleep. My litheless body,
coiled and snug, could've,
once again, fired the hearth
of your quivering waist.

BOB HICOK

Killing

As a boy I killed to kill, clubbed frogs
on the banks of a polluted river
as their knobby eyes protruded
through the foam of filth; turned sun
on ants, magnified Sol to fire, stalked them
with the glass as they scuttled to escape
my God-sized wrath. And if allowed a gun,
a .22 like Todd Clayton and Eric Granger had,
I'd have shot squirrels and jays, possum
and possibly Calvin Jamison as they did once,
in the leg and shoulder because he lisped,
played piano and spoke French, though primarily
because it occurred to them they could.
What changed my habits was a kick
in the ribs one lunch, more so the laughter
of those circling the fight, an impromptu ring,
and the words of the victor, who leaned low
and whispered that he owned my ass,
his face animated by a virulent form of bliss.
He was like linebackers I'd know later
who were calmed by violence, tackles
at peace only when the game was over
and there was blood on their jersey,
an ache where they'd been kneed or bit
and the memory in their flesh
of smashing against another body,
of screaming through a sweep as the play
collapsed around a common intention,
the need to compel others to do what they
didn't want to. I still know some of these guys
and the greatest compliment they can pay's
to say of an old opponent

that he killed them. This usually comes
after a few beers and the acknowledgement
that things aren't like they used to be,
knees and waists, hairlines and music,
which like philosophy is always said
to have been more authentic in the past.
I try to hurt nothing now, not centipede
or toad, the bats which get into the house
and circle in panic, unable to hear
a way out. Not because I'm good but because
the thought never leaves my body,
the child's lesson that not only
can I kill but will and want to.

Rednecks

Gaithersburg, Maryland

At Scot Gas, Darnestown Road,
the high school boys
pumping gas
would snicker at the rednecks.
Every Saturday night there was Earl,
puckering his liquor-smashed face
to announce that he was driving
across the bridge, a bridge spanning
only the whiskey river
that bubbled in his stomach.
Earl's car, one side crumpled like his nose,
would circle slowly around the pumps,
turn signal winking relentlessly.

Another pickup truck morning,
and rednecks. Loitering
in our red uniforms, we watched
as a pickup rumbled through.
We expected: "Fill it with no-lead, boy,
and gimme a cash ticket."
We expected the farmer with sideburns
and a pompadour.
We, with new diplomas framed
at home, never expected the woman.
Her face was a purple rubber mask
melting off her head, scars rippling down
where the fire seared her freak face,
leaving her a carnival where high school boys
paid a quarter to look, and look away.

No one took the pump. The farmer saw us standing
in our red uniforms, a regiment of illiterate conscripts.
Still watching us, he leaned across the seat of the truck
and kissed her. He kissed her
all over her happy ruined face, kissed her
as I pumped the gas and scraped the windshield
and measured the oil, he kept kissing her.

The Lost Underwear of Central Park

Pushing aside stiff panties
with his stick
the old man, stabbing
cans, moves closer
to the trembling wool coat,
gnawed bare in spots,
a patched dress,
hitched up around her hips.

He watches her hand
in its private shiver
and the furious rocking
that lifts her
into the secret palace
of lost pleasures
beyond the bone cold planks
of the thumping bench.

By the cinder path
he spikes a Stroh's.
In bruised flamingo light
he watches ducks unfold,
remembers a pair
of silk stockings once,
caught by the wind,
a lake where he saw

their swiveled dance,
how they arced and fluttered,
the flaming hair laced
with fragrance of jasmine, gin,
how it whipped wildly

like a nameless animal
into his face,
a perfumed sting

and the dance of her eyes
reflecting the slipping away
of the day, wet green
going wet gray.
Slowly he turns from darkening water,
the illusive silk legs
that loop and tangle in his mind
forever kicking up and away.

JOSEPHINE REDLIN

All the Carefully Measured Seconds

Back then I still believed it was possible
to prevent certain things, until that hot afternoon.
It was the middle of grain harvest, August of '54,
when Fred climbed down from his stalled combine
and took off for Montrose to buy a part.
Later I realized the part was a ruse of fate, like
something made up to get someone to a surprise party.
So many times I reran those last hours,
adding or subtracting a few seconds here or there.
Lingering a moment in the field, he could have
noticed the grain shiver as a cloud passed by,
he could have paused by the barn to admire the blue
and lavender flecks adorning the pigeons' throats,
he could have stopped by the house to finger
the soft leaves of the African violets
on the sill, he could have slipped his arm
around Ella's waist as she stood at the sink,
her hands in the dishwater.
But, he swatted the grain dust from his overalls
and climbed into his green Buick to keep
his appointment on Highway 38. Even then,
it was not too late. He could have floored
the car just this once, he could have let
the wind rush in, raising his sparse strands
of matted hair to dance in the breeze.

When I saw Fred's car again, it looked as if
it had been punched by the fist of some god
though surely not the same one who keeps
the earth spinning, the sun and moon rising,
passion ascending to fuse new life,

the rose unfolding with tenderness,
the worm tilling the orchard floor,
all the carefully measured seconds
adding up exactly to us.

Giving Thanks

for Angie and Darrell

Our family came west from the plains;
theirs came north from the desert.
We met as neighbors at the intersection
of aircraft factories and the Pacific Ocean
in Hawthorne, California.
"Join us for Thanksgiving," they said.

My husband and I and our two kids crossed
the street with a platter of apple strudel
and they made room. Grace was said in Spanish.
Wineglasses danced toasts with the rhythm
of a cha-cha: *Adelante...Arriba...Chupa, chupa.*
We had never seen corn husks on the table,
stained orange, plump with filling.
My five-year-old poked at her tamale with
a finger, then looked at me for instructions.
Hot peppers were chomped like celery,
disappearing in the middle of a sentence.
Their eyes met as we sprinkled sugar
on sliced tomatoes.

After dinner the men stepped outside
to smoke and inspect someone's new truck.
The women did the dishes, shared recipes.
I confessed how I had agonized that morning
over the strudel dough, wondering if I
was stretching it too much or not enough.
Carmen patted my shoulder and said,
"Just remember, the important thing
is to make things with a good heart."

Later, everyone retired to the living room
where laughter and voices rose like

the volume slowly turned up on a radio.
Faces and walls took on the reflected
glow of a hearth though the room had none.
Our kids joined their kids running in and out,
showing off kittens clinging to their chests.

At dusk, the room deflated.
Morning would bring early rising
for work in foundries and grinding shops.
As our family walked home in the light rain,
I held tightly to the platter filled
with Angie's turkey, Shelley's Jell-O,
Rudy's salsa, and Carmen's beans.

Strip Joint

"...I once took him to the train station
in Minden, seventy miles away from our home,
and the trains only go through Nebraska at night,
the middle of the night, cause they plan it that way,
cause I suppose Nebraska's a dark passage no one wants
to make awake and so I went with him and we got
there an hour early so no way would any dark train be
sneakin in without our knowing, nothin was gonna
come out of nowhere without our knowing,

so we went to find some place to eat
and the only place open was a bar so we
were just about to devour our hamburgers,
when *she* came onstage, a woman, probably the
only woman in Minden, and she started
dancin for the twenty, maybe thirty men who were
still up and about in Minden at that time of night—

Well, my son and me, we chewed our hamburgers
and I couldn't help but duck a bit when her top
came off and I tried not to look at my son but I
couldn't look at her either so I stared at my hamburger
until I noticed no one else was lookin at the woman cause
they were starin at a TV set above the bar,
a black and white one too, strange in itself,
until I saw it was the bar's surveillance camera
pointed at the stage but even so

I couldn't figure out why they were
starin at the TV instead of her.
Maybe everyone was tryin to be polite,
or maybe everybody's seen a naked dancin woman

in the flesh but no had really seen one
dancin naked on a black and white screen,
or maybe when a TV's on you can't help watchin it,
and who knows what the woman thought of all this.
She just danced, and we just ate, after
a time it didn't even seem like she was there...."

RICHARD GARCIA

Certain Images, Excluded from My Poems, Form a Parade

When the iceberg pulled by a team of white horses comes sliding
down the boulevard, the crowd, which had been so festive,
whistling, hooting, throwing their hats in the air, grows silent.

Almost silent are the ten Kikuyu warriors striding in slow
        motion,
one clenched fist shooting up in the air every ten paces as they
        expel
a loud hiss in unison, making a sizzling sound, like the shallow
rush of sea that slides onto the beach in between waves.

Faint at first then louder is the one-two, one-two-three
clack of the milkmaids, each tapping a wooden ladle against
a wooden pail, their faces flushed, braids stiff with desert dust,
blue eyes fixed on the horizon, as if they could see
a snow-covered peak taking shape in the haze.

Here comes a float that represents the remains of a regiment of
        Assyrian
infantry that disappeared in a sandstorm three thousand years
        ago.
Their spear tips, protruding from the dunes, shine like mica.
And a classical motif, The Three Fates, symbolized by a waitress,
a bank teller, and a meter maid, flinging candies wrapped in foil,
dollar bills and parking tickets at the spectators.

Who is it that comes more splendidly arrayed than the rest,
gold buckles on black velvet sashes, silver badges shining in the
        sun?
It is the poets, a contingent from the Emily Dickinson Brigade
of the Chaparral Society, quite impressive as they drop

to one knee in unison and rap against the blacktop with their
    batons.

Should we join the parade, take up the rear and follow? Who can
    resist
the young Chinese girl, in the black leather mini-skirt, pounding,
slowly pounding on her bass drum, boom-boom, boom-boom-
    boom,
her knees high-stepping to the rhythm, as she leads us
down concrete stairs into the basement of the art museum,
down among the gray columns and rectangular pools of still
    water?

Storm

No coat, bad shoes, caught sudden
In a spring downpour, a girl scrambles
Into a small market on her way
Home from school. The old man is alone,
Picking bruised apples from a bin, tossing them

Softly, one at a time into a slop can.
Usually, he chases kids out, having caught them lifting
Chocolate bars and cigarettes often enough, but today
He looks up, smiles a little, glances away
From the glass doors darkened

By sheeting rain, and the girl feels safe, begins
Leafing through a slick magazine
From the rack. At the next flash and crack
Of thunder, the old man walks to the door, presses
Both fleshy hands to the glass

And asks softly if the girl has ever been
To California. He says he and his wife saved all their lives
To go to the ocean. Then he says she died last week.
The girl doesn't know what to do—
He isn't even looking at her—hair dripping

Onto her shoulders, the damp arms
Of her shirt clinging to her skin—he seems to be speaking
Through the dark glaze, straight into the storm.
He tells how it happened: a slight headache,
A couple of aspirin, how she wiped crumbs

From the kitchen table and checked the stove before going
With him to bed. Then there was that odd sound

In the night—something like a cough. And the cold morning
Realization that he had slept right through
Her leaving. The girl doesn't want to hear this.

The little store has become close, steamy,
Air thick with the slop bucket's ripeness.
The old man's trousers are too baggy and short,
And one brown sock droops down
Around the top of its shoe, a dull rubber-soled oxford.

Rain seeps in onto the floor, glistening
At his feet. *How far away is California?* the girl asks, twisting
At a page in her magazine. He turns, his face glowing
Against the door. She is thirteen. She's never
Seen a man cry before, and he moves slowly

Toward her, his hands reaching out
Like a blind man, mouth open, making
A kind of moan. She takes his hands, lets him fall
To his knees, unbutton her wet shirt, and press
His burning face to her heart.

Reconciliation

Angry at my persistent rejection of what he said
Was his love, a skinny neighborhood boy
Once held his mother's kitchen knife

To my twelve-year-old throat. This comes to mind
Today as I walk past a couple of tough teenage boys
Near the local high school, dressed in the same

Oversized black shirts and backwards-turned
Baseball caps, gliding down the busy street so close
Together, it's as if they are dancing—in love

With the nearness of each other and the respect
They seem to elicit from the crowd, as it parts
And rejoins in their wake.

After a party, the boy followed my friend and me
Across a vacant field and along the dark railroad tracks
Toward my house. He stood behind me, one arm rough

Around my chest, the other holding the blade's edge
Against my skin. I could smell
Tobacco on his fingers and sweat and something

Like oil or tar from the tracks, and I could hear him breathing
Hard into my ear between words. I'd never been so close
To a boy before, and I believed I was going to die.

It wasn't that I was especially new
To danger—I don't remember ever knowing
That naive invulnerability children are said to feel.

It was the confusing connection of force
And love that I still find so disturbing.
I consented without hesitation

To everything he asked, making a scared humming sound
To show agreement. I'd dance with him, I'd go
To the movies with him, I'd kiss him, I'd hold hands

With him in front of everyone at school. He had made himself
The center of my life. My girlfriend must have been there
Somewhere—maybe she ran screaming

For help, or maybe she stood crying, helpless, watching
From a safe distance—after thirty years I can't even
Recall her name. All I can think of is the hard metal buttons

Of his denim jacket, jabbing into my back, his hips
Pushing at me awkwardly from behind, the scratchy
Sound of his voice, his left hand ripping

Open my cotton shirt and groping
At my still boyish chest. What had I done
To make him want to hurt me? And what did this scene

Of romantic terror have to do with love—or desire?
I believe he wanted to kill me. I understood even then
That he was a disturbed and angry child,

But I've never been able to clarify
My own part in the picture. I know the dangers
Of blaming the victim, and I've been advised

Repeatedly to avoid taking responsibility
For the actions of others. But those mental health boundaries
Somehow seem too neatly drawn. Every morning

Washing my face, my fingertips find the narrow ridge
Of white scar tissue on my neck where his sharp knife
Drew blood, and I realize I was lucky

To survive. I've hated him for many years, hated
The absolute power of that knife
In his hand. But until that night, I'd actually been

Slightly flattered by all the attention: the candy bars
Left in my desk, the phone calls, the obsessive notes
Slipped into my locker and pinned

To my door at home. For the first time in my life,
The other girls circled around me, outraged
At the nerve of such a friendless and undesirable boy,

But impressed, nevertheless, by the passion
Of his persistence. The need
To feel wanted was at work all around,

And at that young age, it was a heady exercise
Of power to reject him. I wonder
If he ever thinks of this. The daily news tells me

About children murdering parents, abusing
And raping other children, and the question of who
Is responsible for what becomes a nightmarish attempt

To untangle the tightly knotted lives of everyone
Involved. I don't mean to forgive him.
Forgiveness, like blame or praise, seems to assume

The existence of the pure individual, and at this point
In my own impure life I've come to doubt
Such a tidy monster exists.

I admit there have been times I've wanted
To force someone to love me—and I suppose
It's even possible that force might be effective

In a world where love is nothing more or less
Than dependence, and respect is defined primarily by fear.
After all these years, I can't think of that boy without feeling

The clear shape of his body behind me, insistent
As a shadow, grasping for what might be
The only dance there is.

Whoa

I can taste that tongue for me you've set to rubbing in your
  pocket
Like a stone excited cricket, flint you'll strike when right in
  moonsteam: blue

Glue, apogee, cunt of night. Coyotes, a fire round in a ground.
Much hair is all of your black bones suckling
Open in my throat all ready. Why don't you stick that brilliant

Strop, heartboot into my speechless pickup? I want you as a
  woman
With a man wants a woman: thick wet neck to drive on, one
  full dark week naked,
Stung. And stinging, sniffing cells through bruises;
Stinking, ochre-dusted limbs. Notice how the desert

Arson fits us like a cave tonight. Listen
To the fetal flex, my larval only opal. Smell

It? Whisper my, my creosote. Be my salmon Jesus.
At dawn, nuzzled jaw to thigh, jacketed coiler, *please* us. O my
Shotgun, now, now. Soon can skin sing where,

Here? Clutch
Unforgotten, button of blood. O currency: the ring around.
  The moon, and its satellite
Night. Kiss long this maddening, stalling stillness. Low, watch
  the ground mouth *move.*

Analogue

*…only making love to you wasn't I
curious about the rest of experience…*
—Jane Miller

once i snake my
dress off i will loll
still as volts
train my feet to paint
opposing murals
if a riff of flesh
will halve me
on this tasty day
in the luxurious barren
of your psychedelicious
desert, honey
artist of most succulent
structures
& o i shed my cells
all right, o electric
storm of lips
osmosis of my groin
here your fingers
manufacture
thunder from my pillow
& startle my bone
of your body
with sheer volume
of antediluvian ocean affection
physiospiritual
hieroglyphic bee
impending thrust of yellow dust
exploding moon of day
water-colored ever for
the pool of sands between me

Mayela One Day in 1989

I'm in a city called El Paso. I could point it out on a map. Right here, here it is. There is longitude, latitude. For most, this is enough, a satisfactory explanation. But say we don't use all these imaginary concepts. Say there is no west of or east of or north of or south of. Forget all that. Forget these legalistic boundaries. No Texas here, no Mexico there, no New Mexico. Forget all that. Here's a river. Here are mountains. A sky above. Night, day. Sun and moon. Where there are people, there are buildings, and streets, and walkways. There are colorful and not so signs with messages that can be reduced to words. Eat. Sleep. Money. Work. Play. Away from those, and away from the buildings and people, the brown soil is a rock even at its surface. The vegetation is sparse, gray-green, low to the ground, defensive. There is little water away from that river.

I walk on the streets. Or drive. Think about what I did before. How maps worked. I would open them and trace a road and I'd get there and I'd think I had discovered something, that I knew where I was. I'd go into a bar. Sit on a stool facing mirrors reflecting mirrors and bottles and think how this offered not just solace but solution. Or drugs. Or love. Or sex. I remember when I'd meet a woman. The old answer, the first answer. Find a woman, lose myself through a woman, find myself: Here I am.

Only a thick pane of glass and a sidewalk away, she's been glancing back at me—isn't she?—as she talks to a gray-haired man with a luxury car. She's huskier than him, a few inches taller, and as dramatic and endowed as fantasy: it's her red dress and wavy black hair and a blue, cloudless sky, as Mexican as cheap paint, that halos her, and a nasty kink in her eyes which I can see even at this distance.

She is sitting across the booth I'm in. Her name is Mayela. We are in a coffee shop downtown where sunburned truck drivers talk the loudest in drawling English, tattoos on their hairy arms, wearing cowboy hats. Women, having lunch, wear nylons and high heels and imitation pearl necklaces. The coffee is too hot, too old, too black, too thin, and I color it with the white liquid that isn't milk. The waitress has a bun of hair bobby-pinned to the top of her head, two cloth flowers stitched into the net containing the bun. The mix is fertile and intoxicating, though like a drug cut with strychnine, there is an edge on the rush, a rustling breeze of death, and the whirl makes bold the blood and breath and muscle. When it has become later, the same restaurant, the sky blue-red, too bright and gaudy to be anywhere else but here, there is no one else, not even the waitress pouring more coffee, and now she, not us, is the phantasm.

Mayela tells stories of men: fathers, brothers, cousins, lovers. Mayela has a husband. He lives in Houston, a dangerous American town where he left her by herself too often. She could not be alone like that, she says, as if of no more or less importance, and she never loved him. She only wanted to get away any way she could. Hers wasn't a home, that mud building near Chihuahua. It was her grandfather's house, and she slaved there, cleaning this, raking that, cooking, washing, nursing a grandmother and younger, fatherless children that were brother or half-sister or cousin or niece, and, then, also her mother. Her mother stopped being well for so long that one day, Mayela says, she couldn't be sure she was awake or asleep. So she married, at sixteen, and she had two children, and now she is here because she never loved that man. She cannot find a lover who can satisfy her. She is tormented by lovers. One, at twenty-two, is younger than her. Another, her boyfriend, is thirty-five, and he sometimes wants too much from her—he throws things, and she doesn't know about him, and so she won't see him for days and sometimes weeks. The man with gray hair, almost sixty, treats her with elegance and dances with her in the middle of the day where lights are under the floor and tells her how to be near her is all he might ever ask for. He gave her a car, a used sports car. He says she can have a house that will be hers, and he will carry the note. Mayela says she took the car but will pay for it and that she won't take the house. Because there's always payments.

I tell her how I feel sorry for her because a woman like her cannot live simply. She is monitored, never ignored. She is supposed to be stronger and more resistant than a man. Men always approaching her, making conversation supposed to not be about what it is. So many men, so much temptation. Too many temptations. Leaning toward her, making my voice as close as I want my body, I whisper *this, us,* that even as these words leave my lips, as my hands would move over her body, it is not me at all but *her,* that I am the one drawn in, that I will be the one caught and that she will be the one who has led me here. You, I tell Mayela, are temptress, and I am prey.

After we've sat for a while at a bar, after several mixed drinks, she suggests where we go next. It doesn't matter to me because I am with her and there is no better or worse.

We drive past the lights and the well-known streets. Past the old courthouse and the new jail into the dark, oldest part of town, where frail tenements are without plumbing or electricity, where the Spanish language is spoken in its most idiomatic form, so close to roots of meaning and sound that words breed like simple cells. Dark, so dark that stars glare like streetlights, while the moon hovers as in wilderness. Through this sludge of night, we cross dead, metal ribs of train tracks, warehouses whose signs are brushed over chipping plaster and brick as frequently as gang tags. We glimpse bars whose decor and patrons—like the jukebox boasts and cries of love and death seeming to push open their doors—are as elemental as horses and goats and snakes, as leather and lard, as sweat and sunburn and rocks. We search these dark night streets with the simplest of names—First, Second, Third— because Mayela has forgotten, until we are there. Right there, look, where so many cars are innocently parked. At a corner. A yellow light over the door. Its name is above that light and can't be read easily: The Old Dominion.

I am with Mayela, and she has brought me here, and I hold her hand, and she grips mine in return. It is hot outside, hotter inside, and the music is full of rhythmic bass and pulsates like a drug against the glassy eyes of the men, so many men. No, they are not exactly the eyes of men, and they are not exactly the eyes of women. One walks by in pants that are more a dress and a puffy shirt that is more a blouse, and has long, straightened black hair but also a full-faced, trimmed beard. The rest are not so metaphorical. This is not a club to show off clothes or styles, not for satin or silk or suede, not animal-skin boots or brimmed hats. Only essences of style, what can survive in this desert, in the deepest West of all, where few things, or people, prosper.

I am holding Mayela's hand as she leads me past all of them for a space to stop and lean. Flesh is the steam of the club, the expiring hot moisture. Flesh. It's what I'm here for. There is no difference between them and me in this. Mayela stops, and I remain very close to her.

These men want men in the Old Dominion and don't pretend indifference, don't disguise. And some women who want women, too, and before several pass us, they slow down, then from toe to head and mostly in between, imagine Mayela. Mayela offers no reward for their attentions. They look at me and wink, raise eyebrows, hand-signal approval and envy. We are the most obvious here. Mayela is a large, tall woman, and full, and I stand over her in cowboy boots.

Mayela says something I don't hear over the pounding amps. The club is too crowded, and it is dirty, the brown, ever-blowing desert on the rug, bar, dance floor, even the moistened air is a dusty fog. A man approaches Mayela. They hug, then talk into each other's ears, then she indicates for me to guard the drink I've bought her, then goes with him to the smooth floor in front of us. She dances without excess, with contented movements. The man twirls and spins around her, laughing, gesticulating, his hips and arms seductive, suggestive, very close to her body. Mayela's modest grin is constant and cooperative. I am drinking too much, and it, too, disorients me. I order another for myself. I am remembering where I am. I am with Mayela, who is dancing with another man.

There are metal poles at the corners of the dance floor. They are bolted at the floor and ceiling. A few feet up, a crude platform circles each, and a muscular male dancer in a G-string undulates against his pole, rolling against and around it, riding, humping. It is a strain, frightening, because I don't want to see everything, and I fear the scoring on my psyche. Beneath the G-string are men, not women, men who are running their hands up and down the platform dancer, squeezing, caressing his calves and thighs and ass as he slides and rubs the pole between his legs, eyes closed in rapture. It is like my sexual yearning, only played out by a naked man against a pole with other men running their hands over him. Then again, no: when I want a woman, I want that one woman and not any woman, not Woman.

And Mayela is still dancing, though the man has left her. Now she is with a woman, and they are the only women on the dance floor, and the men are watching the two of them, and now I am watching them watch. In this heat they are sweating, their skin a milky pallor, thick and sticky.

I'm rubbing Mayela's neck while she listens to the woman she danced with. I want to feel her body, and I want to leave. I'm shaken, I'm drunk. She reaches around, touches my hand, but she has to listen to what I cannot hear. So I finish another drink.

Then we are on the dance floor, at the center, because Mayela has insisted on taking it. We are the spectacle, we are the couple. At the perimeters are the men, and those few women, seeing us, detailing. Mayela is circling me, her dress, yellow as sunshine, at once whirling away and clinging to her body. Hers is not a show for me, and not a show for them. It is for herself, as unconscious as trance. I'm miserable until I realize it is only the phantasm, and I am free. I am with Mayela. I am the man with Mayela.

Todd, it is explained, is a friend of Mayela's friend, the man she'd danced with. He is young, maybe twenty-one, and he knows Mayela from before. Todd, which is his favorite name, has bleached blond hair that is cut stylishly short. It is moussed, he tells us. Todd has drawn the faintest of purple lines around his dark black Mexican eyes. We are outside the club, leaning against parked cars, smoking marijuana. It's late. It is still dark, the only light the dim one above the club entrance facing the other street. Power lines drape over us, linked from one wooden pole to another, hanging above buildings, going in here and there, never visibly ending. Swamp coolers stand on top of the roofs waiting for daylight. It is dark except for the hot cherry of the joint and Mayela's yellow dress and Todd's white shirt buttoned to the top, and stars that remind us the desert is beneath and around us, and the moon, and the red square taillights becoming smaller on the street's horizon until they are no more.

Todd has been cruising several guys this evening. He doesn't know which will work out for him. He has split with Mayela's friend. She understands about him, he tells her.

He talks with a need to, and Mayela and I must listen to him. Mayela asks about his brother. He has tested positive, Todd says, but he doesn't have it yet, it is still dormant. He takes pills he gets in Juárez, Todd says. It is quiet and so hot, even with a breeze. His brother still likes to dress up, Todd says. He puts on a dress and goes out. He wants to have the operation but how, and, with this disease possibility, he is in a panic. He is so scared and lost and confused, Todd explains. It is quiet except when someone else enters or exits the club and the music pours out, jackhammering the sidewalk and asphalt. And then suddenly Todd changes his mood and pitch. His brother's such a whore, and he wants to live as much as he can *now*! And then, as abruptly, Todd drops this subject and begins to talk about himself and the man he is most interested in tonight.

Stop. I have to leave. We have to go.

I'm not sure where I'm driving, but we are back in the lights of downtown, away from the stars. I'm telling Mayela that it was, it was, that I was trying. She says she's used to it. And she likes these men. They are a challenge to her, she says.

A challenge? The car windows are down, and the wind, like the heat, is an unmistakable presence.

For example, she says, her friend. Who is Todd's friend. She knows he wanted her. Tonight when she was dancing, the woman, she knew that woman wanted her. But so did he. Did I notice? She says she always knows these women want her, but her satisfaction comes from knowing she has attracted a man like Todd's friend, because he doesn't want women. Only a special woman. She *knew*, she tells me brightly, proud, that he wanted her. Did I understand how she knew?

I see the dancer in the G-string riding that pole.

Mayela's face is the color of a kiln-dried, earthen mask. Her nose is broad, her cheeks are high, her eyes slant and are as dark as love and fear. Mayela is not only beautiful. Only I don't know the mythology, I don't know the gods or the demons.

I am alert, and I remember where I am going: to the bar where she parked the sports car her gray-haired man gave her.

You think I'm a lesbian? she asks, noticing my shift.

I'm imagining Todd's brother in a dress. Or I'm imagining her riding the metal pole between her legs. I can't think of what to say, though, so I don't say anything. And I'm not sure about what she is asking me.

Well, I'm not, she tells me. She, too, distances, seems confused.

I stop in the parking lot next to her sports car. I turn my head toward her, and say, This is when it's supposed to be the good night kiss, isn't it?

We don't *kiss* good night, she informs me, both mad and hurt.

We. I see Todd's friend rubbing himself against her on the dance floor.

Good night.

Slowly she opens the door for herself. Slowly she walks to her own car. I wait, politely, for her to get inside, to start the motor.

I am in El Paso. It is 1989.

THOMAS BELLER

Nondestructive Testing

One day Will arrived at work to find a new receptionist sitting behind the front desk, and all that morning he found himself contemplating his brief glimpse of her. She was a large woman, not just in size but also in the boldness of her features— her eyes were big and blue, her cheeks were daubed in bright rouge, her lips were red and full. Moving between his desk to the bathroom and back, Will showered her with glances, but offered just a flicker of a smile.

More than a mere convenience, the office bathroom was a sanctuary for Will. He would sit down in one of the stalls, rest his head in his arms, and listen to the quiet groaning of the skyscraper's plumbing. It was a very modern building on Fifty-second Street, a thin streak of black poking aggressively into the sky. On stormy days Will sat for long periods of time and listened to it sway.

Will worked at a bank, in a small esoteric subdivision which monitored the activities of other banks. He was a permanent temp, a condition that suited him, as this was not his intended career. He had just dropped out of divinity school at Yale when he took the job, and he was only going to keep it until he could figure out what he was going to do next. Gradually, however, what he was doing now and what he was going to do next merged into the same thing. His job was similar to that of a monk copying scripture by hand, except in this case what he was copying were loan agreements acquired by some sleight of hand from another bank. It was supposed to take six months. A year had passed, and no end was in sight. The corporate salesmen in the office had caught his eye. They were cheerful, energetic men in well-tailored suits whose arrivals and departures were always accompanied by great flurries of activity, and he felt a twinge of admiration for them. Something crass and materialistic was stirring within him, and he vaguely enjoyed the thought that it might be his fate to be rich, to be a mover and shaker, a man of surfaces.

His reasons for dropping out of divinity school were complicated, and he had a hard time explaining them to the many people who were confused and concerned by his decision, including his girlfriend, Liza, who shortly thereafter became his ex-girlfriend. The best analogy he could come up with was that of a musician who is suddenly gripped by performance anxiety and no longer wants to play his instrument before an audience—the audience in this case being God. In fact, he had come to the private conclusion that there was no audience.

All morning a parade of people came in and out of the office, most of them welcoming the new receptionist warmly, some just nodding. If someone got a call and wasn't at his or her desk, she got to page the person over the office intercom. Every few minutes she would have her own mini-performance for an audience of about forty. Several fashion magazines lay on her desk alongside a bulky copy of the score of *La Traviata*. She was looking at one of the magazines when she first met Will, who was returning from yet another trip to the men's room.

"Did I get any calls just now?" he said brusquely.

"Um, you're ..."

"Will. Hi." He smiled for a moment.

"No, no calls, Will." His name came off her tongue with something approaching familiarity. She spoke slowly and her words had just a hint of a Southern accent around the edges.

"Oh," he said, staring at her thoughtfully. "Good." He was of medium build with dark hair and thin black eyebrows that were just slightly askance, giving him a perpetually expectant look.

"Well, Will," she said. "I'm Marla. And how are you doing today?"

"Fine," he said, and then added, "Bored. Extremely bored. I can't even tell you."

"You don't have to," she said. "What I'm doing isn't exactly fascinating, either. But ..."—and here she sighed in a somewhat dramatic manner—"it gets me through school."

"School?" he said, raising his eyebrows as though it were a piece of slang he hadn't yet heard.

"I'm here to study opera at the Juilliard School of Music," she said brightly. "I've already performed down in Austin, where I'm from."

Something about her enthusiasm embarrassed him—suddenly he was very self-conscious of his hands. "That's nice," he said, and turned to go back into the office.

"Seen the new receptionist?" Will said to his co-worker, Hoffman.

Their desks faced each other in a small fluorescent-lit room. The vice president in charge of the division—a loud, over-friendly man whose ambition was as evident as a dog's lust while it humps someone's leg—had come up with what he considered a snappy title for their project: "Info-War." Among the two soldiers, however, moral was low.

"Yup. Saw her," said Hoffman, and didn't move his eyes from the page in front of him.

"She's really quite, you know..." Will paused, trying to figure out just what word he was looking for. "Nice," he said finally, though this wasn't what he meant. "Nice" was the word for everyone else in the office, the kind of "Let's just be nice to one another so we can get through this damn situation, all right?" brand of friendliness that Will despised. Marla was something else. "She's an opera singer," he said. "Did you know that? And from Texas. An aspiring opera star from Texas."

When Hoffman made no response, Will stared at him, at the clean creases of his dress shirt, the tight knot of his tie, and the miraculous dimple it created just below, which, despite hours of rehearsal in front of a mirror, Will had not been able to duplicate. Hoffman was one of those men who seem to have been born with an innate understanding of how to choose a suit, how to knot a tie, how to walk around with a cool, handsome expression that would be as appropriate for an office party as it would for foreclosing on a family farm. Will had taken great satisfaction in Hoffman's one discernible flaw: a skin problem of some sort on his right index finger, which left it dry and scaly and which had prompted the fingernail to attempt an evacuation. Will would stare at that finger, mesmerized as it made the small squiggly motion of handwriting, and imagine what internal terrors it represented.

It was the morning of Marla's arrival that Hoffman, with the air of someone involved in high-level espionage, announced his plans to leave the company and start his own business, a newsletter that reported on the nondestructive testing industry.

"I didn't know you could test destructively," said Will.

"Nondestructive testing is a way of testing things like airplanes and nuclear reactors without actually taking them apart, or trying to damage them to see if they hold up," said Hoffman. "It uses ultrasonic waves, infrared light, radiology, things like that. It's the testing of the future. There's no harm."

"Experiments with no risk," Will said. He liked the metaphysical possibilities for something like this. His life had been full of tests and experiments, and most of them, it seemed, had been fairly destructive. A year and a half earlier, he had had a career and a girlfriend, for example, and now he had neither.

At three o'clock Will was seized with a desperate craving for something sweet. It was as instinctive as the odd habit he had of waking up one minute before his alarm went off every morning. He fiercely tried to resist, but to no avail, and every day he made a pilgrimage to the lobby newsstand to buy a candy bar. On his way out today, he paused, quite impulsively, in front of Marla.

"How're you doing?" he said, cheered by the sight of her. He caught himself in the ridiculous arabesque pose he sometimes affected when he was trying to imply that he had been up late the preceding night doing something fabulously interesting. He corrected himself immediately and stood up straight.

"Just fine," she said, and her voice filled the room. It was clear, friendly, melodious, and slightly melodramatic—the kind of voice that would be equally appropriate for the evening news or phone sex. All day he had been listening to it page people over the office intercom. He smiled at her.

She smiled back. Her skin was smooth and clear except for a faint birthmark just below her left temple, the color and shape of a coffee stain.

He stood there struggling for something to say. After a few seconds, he just nodded and turned to go downstairs for his candy bar. He rode down with an attractive woman whose prim, constrained manner seemed like an active rebellion against her pretty features and full hips. In this regard she reminded him of Liza, who was always worried about her weight, in spite of the fact she had a lovely figure. He had teased her that no matter how much weight she lost, she would always have a nice juicy ass for everyone to see. He told her that he had been fat when he was younger and she was so amused by this, and amazed, since he showed no signs of it now, that she started calling him Fatty, until he asked her very seriously to stop. He saw his early fatness as a kind of purgatory through which he had suffered, and the thought of what he had endured in grade school still made him shudder.

When he returned to the office, Marla was handling several calls at once. The switchboard was filled with blinking red lights. Her large fingers with their bright red nail polish poked at the tiny buttons, and her face had a look of confused concentration—the blank expression of the kid in a seventh grade spelling bee who, when confronted with the word "friend," is stumped. He had been that kid. Her lips were slightly parted, red and glossy, turned down a bit at the corners.

He imagined something white and sticky splattering across that open mouth. The image arrived with such sudden intensity that he turned the corner into the office area with a slightly shocked look on his face, as though he had just stepped over a pornographic photo lying face-up on the street.

The next day Will arrived in his usual morning stupor and flew past Marla with hardly a nod. He was late, and the vice president had recently posted a letter in the office lunchroom that read: "I have noticed an increase in tardiness among the staff. THIS WILL STOP." Against all rationality, Will suspected the vice president was making a subliminal communication to him. On that particular day, the vice president was in one of his hands-on, loiter-around-the-little-people moods, and so Will had to forgo his bathroom respites. He worked right through lunch. He couldn't get away until midafternoon, and by then he had completely forgotten about Marla. Her voice, normally so musical and intriguing to him when it wafted over the intercom, had become part of the background drone of the office.

When he saw her, he came up short. She was wearing a very sharp two-piece jacket-and-skirt outfit with a checkered pattern, and a white dress shirt with some frills around the collar. Her light brown hair was pulled in a knob-like bun behind her head, and a few minor curls escaped around her neck. It was the Female Executive as Impersonated by Receptionist look.

"Hi, there," she said. "Where've you been?"

"Drowning," he said.

"I didn't know there was a pool back there," she said. "I'll have to bring my bathing suit."

Will's mind, enfeebled by the grueling day, was not ready for this abstraction. He abruptly turned and started to head for his candy bar. Then he had a strange impulse and turned around to face Marla.

"Do you have any candy?" he asked.

"Candy?" she said. He was about to turn away and head downstairs when her face performed one of its dramatic changes; it took on the expression of a shoplifter caught red-handed.

"Yes, I do," she said with a slightly confessional fervor, and started to rummage around the large leather bag that served as her purse. "Here." She held out a small white paper bag. "Take the whole thing. I don't want any. I shouldn't have even bought them."

Will walked over and took the bag from her. She seemed relieved to have it out of her hand. It was half full.

He looked at her with a slightly confused expression, not understanding her urgency.

"Really, please take it all, I shouldn't have even bought it."

In that short sentence, Will found more emotion than anything he had heard uttered at work in the year he had been there, and he found his sudden proximity to a human being at once exhilarating and distasteful. Inside the bag was a small cache of little coffee bean–shaped chocolates. They were the sort of candy his grandmother used to have in a bowl on the coffee table when he came for a visit. They were bittersweet. They were refined.

"Coffee beans," he said, peering into the bag.

"They're good. They're much better than the Reese's Peanut

Butter Cups and that sort of junk me and my roommate eat most of the time."

"I'll just take one," he said.

"No! Really, take the whole thing."

He took two and handed the bag back to her, pleased at this newfound ability to torture her.

"Thanks," he said. On the way down in the elevator, he ate one; it tasted just as remembered, refined and discrete, bittersweet. He put the other one on his desk, and he glanced at it periodically, the way one might glance at a pebble taken from a beach long ago and remember the whole vacation.

The next day, on his way back from lunch, Will presented Marla with a present.

"I have something for you," he said, and leaned against the wooden counter in front of her.

"You have something for me?" said Marla, and swung her chair around toward him, her voluptuous body performing a kind of twist while seated. Her shoulders and breasts came at him with alarming velocity; her face wore an expression of excited anticipation, as though she were thinking, "What a nice man," but it also had an element of mock surprise, the expression of an adult receiving a present from a little boy.

Their eyes met, and Will stared intently into hers as he swung his arm out from behind his back, a Hershey's chocolate bar sitting in the middle of his pink hand.

Marla bit her lower lip.

"With almonds," he said.

"Oh," she said. "Thank you. That's nice of you."

"Just returning the favor."

"I shouldn't."

"I thought you liked chocolate."

"I love chocolate," she said, "But I shouldn't."

Will almost said, "Why not?" but decided this was too cruel.

"Tell you what," he said. "I'll leave it here, and you can eat it if you want." He put the chocolate bar down right in front of her, smiled, and walked back into his office without saying another word. When he came by later that afternoon, it had disappeared.

He peeked conspicuously at the place where he had left it and then at her.

"Thank you, Will," she said.

This turned into a daily ritual. Will would return from his snack errand and deposit a chocolate bar in front of Marla, who would protest vehemently.

"Don't, please don't," she would say. Or she would say, "You're spoiling me." And once: "You're only doing this because you know I can't resist."

A secretary watched the exchange and said, "How come you keep bringing her candy when she says she doesn't want any?"

Will shrugged. "Maybe she doesn't mean it," he said, to which the secretary responded with a disapproving look.

"Oh, he knows I love it," he heard Marla say as he walked away.

Outwardly, these exchanges resembled the polite, empty cheerfulness that pervaded all the interactions in the office. Will liked that. The surface propriety rendered it a non-event, an exchange that needn't have any consequences, and therefore what happened beneath the surface could go to the farthest extremes.

He imagined her onstage, her full, shapely body and naked optimism the focus of everyone's attention, her mouth issuing a dramatic high-pitched note. It was a stark contrast to the constrained gestures her job required.

He reflected on his own days, their utter mindless monotony, and compared them to the summer after college, when divinity school lay ahead of him. Divinity school had been like a glass elevator that never stopped on any floor, but kept ascending to the greatest heights and descending to the lowest depths and never to any exits. But what had replaced it was a world without elevators, one sprawling single-story structure with no elevation or descent.

But Marla hadn't fully arrived in this structure. She had a certain drive, a willfulness, and he admired it, coveted it, even, and at the same time, felt a desire to crush it that had strange sexual overtones. He debated whether his teasing of her was wrong. He had always liked being tantalized. When he was a kid, his family had always said a long grace before dinner, and though he had found it excruciating, it did—he had to admit—increase his enjoyment of the meal once it finally started. And divinity school was the ultimate tantalization—his gaze focused intently on something he would never see. So, he thought to himself, what was wrong with being the tantalizer for a change? Anyway, he rationalized, it was just a game.

The content of their exchanges slowly evolved. The candy bars were supplemented with gum and other small presents, though it was always something sweet. It was their little secret. She complained to him about not being able to get up from her spot at the switchboard—"I have no mobility," was how she put it—and he asked her questions about growing up in Texas, about opera; he liked listening to her voice.

Her one opportunity for "mobility" came when she made one of several trips during the day from the front desk to the kitchen to refill her plastic Evian bottle with water from the kitchen tap. She tended to use the same bottle for a week at a time, and by the end of the first day, her red lipstick would have tinted the nozzle. For the rest of the week, it sat next to her, its tip bright pink.

Her trip to the kitchen took her past the room where Will and Hoffman worked opposite each other. Will always attempted to look deeply engrossed when she came by. He didn't want Hoffman witnessing their interactions, and also, he liked the idea that what he was doing seemed important.

"You drink a lot of water," he said one day when she returned with a full bottle. Hoffman had stepped away from the desk. She paused next to him. It was the first time she had been standing while he was sitting.

"I'd rather be drinking gin and tonics," she said. She wore that imperious, I'm-too-good-for-this-place expression he liked so much.

"That's my favorite drink," he said.

"We'll have to have one together sometime." As she said this, she casually reached over and stroked Will's hair and part of his neck. It was a mixture of a loving caress and the kind of tousling one gives to a little boy after he's done a good deed. He leaned into it a little, and his eyes took a slow reflexive blink of pleasure, like a cat being petted.

Their eyes met, and Will smiled nervously. He'd never really considered being with her in the real world. The office was an artificial bubble within which they could have their flirtation, and even that was mostly restricted to the transient space of the reception area. If he saw her outside this rigid context, all the rules would change. Everything would be out in the open, beyond his control. They would be together by choice, her presence next to him announcing a conscious sexual preference. He saw himself at a restaurant with her and imagined bumping into a casual acquaintance, perhaps someone from the office. And then, as if to demonstrate what it would be like, Hoffman returned with an amused look on his face. Will stared at him, preparing to hate him if he said something snide, but as soon as she walked away, Hoffman put a large envelope on the desk and removed its contents with the ginger care of a man defusing a bomb.

"I just got the logo design for my newsletter. What do you think?"

He held up a piece of glossy paper.

"The Nondestructive Tester," Will said out loud.

"Well?"

"It has a nice ring to it. *The Nondestructive Tester.* Could be a newsletter for high school teachers specializing in very nervous students."

"I think it speaks right to the client, right to the people who are doing the testing, who are going to want to know the information we provide."

Hoffman's eyes began to shine, and his voice dipped in pitch. This was obviously a speech he was preparing. Will pictured him standing in front of an easel, pointer in hand, making a presentation. The attending businessmen would look at his charts with glazed eyes and then at him, thinking, "How the hell does that guy get his tie to dimple so perfectly?" There was something charming about Hoffman's secret plans. He was like a prisoner unfurling the blueprints of the jail.

"Tester," said Will, musing. "Tester. Sounds a bit like testicle. *The Nondestructive Testicle: A Newsletter for Today's Compassionate Man.*"

Hoffman glared at him and put the secret plans back in their envelope, where they would be retrieved when the time was right.

Shortly after Marla's proposition, Will began to withdraw. It was an impulsive reaction. He did not want this experiment to leave the realm of the hypothetical. He felt it was a deficiency in his personality, like someone who constantly goes to enormous lengths to get to the beach, only to then not go in the water, but he did not question it. He survived his job on the premise that it was temporary; to involve himself with Marla would make it part of his life.

First the candy bars stopped, then the idle banter at the reception area, and finally he began to avoid her glances altogether. Marla reacted to each new development like a dancer who steps forward each time her partner steps away. Her voice was as smooth and rich as ever, but it began to be inflected with recrimination. She could pack the phrase "Good morning, Will" with enough information to make his hands moist. He felt the sting of her disappointment but could think of no course of action other than to hide from it. He occasionally caught her in an expression of wistfulness and felt that he had joined the enormous ranks of people in the world who didn't appreciate her. But his sympathetic feelings were entirely internal, and now he marched past her to the bathroom with hardly a nod, even as those visits had been transformed into brief convulsions of masturbatory pleasure, with her as the subject.

Then one day Marla walked passed his desk and dropped a chocolate bar on it. "Returning the favor," she said, and then walked away.

When the phone rang, Will was in his underwear and socks, pacing around the living room with a gin and tonic. Rock music blared in the background; his work clothes lay crumpled in a chair. This was one of his primary forms of entertainment, having a drink by himself and playing music. It was early in the evening, and he was slightly drunk.

"Will?" Marla's voice wafted over the phone into his ear. It had been nearly two months since she had started working at his company and several weeks since they had stopped talking. He cocked his head, paused, looked around his apartment. He didn't want to answer. There was something gross about her voice intruding into his home. Her voice was the official voice of the workplace.

"Will? Is that you? It's Marla. I'm down at this bar."

"Hold on," said Will, and went to turn the music off. "You're at a bar," he said when he returned.

"Yes. Just a few blocks away from you, as a matter of fact."

"How did you find out where I live?"

"I have my ways." Her voice slurred a little, its Texas accent more pronounced than usual. "Would you like to come join me?"

A picture of her sitting alone at a bar came to him. He imagined what sort of man would try to pick her up. He wondered if this was something she did often, go to bars and get drunk by herself. Half of him wanted to run over and rescue her from what he was picturing, and the other half wanted to slam the phone down in its cradle.

"Why don't you come over here?" he said instead. For a second he wanted to retract it, but it was too late. He listened to his words fly over the phone. "I've got some gin, some tonic..." Happy bar sounds gurgled over the phone like a running tap, but Marla was silent. "Some lime."

"Oh, well, if you have lime..."

She said she would be there in ten minutes.

Will put the phone down and stood still for a few moments.

"You're crazy," he announced to no one, and then without missing a beat, he frantically began to run around the room cleaning up. Tiny gold beads no bigger than a ball bearing were scattered around his apartment, the strange legacy of Liza's last visit, when her necklace broke. He kept thinking he had found the last one, and then another would pop up. He saw one now, glimmering in the corner, and picked it up to examine it. It was like a germ of Liza's presence, and he was reminded of her faintly disapproving manner, the way that their sex life had, after an auspicious beginning, made a slow steady retreat into propriety and then nonexistence. But this was part of his past. He was free of it now, and with his newfound liberty, he decided to do something extravagant and perverse. He was going to buy a chocolate cake. He was going to make Marla take off all her clothes and sit at the kitchen table with a napkin around her neck like a bib. It would come down to the tops of her breasts. Her nipples would bob in and out of sight, and he would feed her chocolate cake with his hands.

He put on his pants and was halfway out the door when he glimpsed his apartment in its disheveled state and was suddenly gripped with the desire to make it nice for Marla. He went back to neatening up.

The doorbell made him jump. He opened the door, and she stood in the doorway, and for a fleeting moment she looked quite small. She was wearing the same outfit she had worn at work that day, a light green skirt and a black long-sleeve shirt with large fake emeralds—blue, green, and red—sewn in around the neck. She stepped inside amidst an invisible cloud of fragrance, what seemed like an entire display counter's worth of perfume.

"It's nice," she said, looking around and taking a deep breath, as though she'd just completed a long trip. "So much room!"

"Really? You must live in a closet."

"I do," she said. "And with a roommate."

Will had planned to escort Marla to the kitchen table, but Marla took matters into her own hands and walked over to the couch, which was old and in bad shape and which made a painful groaning sound when she sank into it.

Will stood nervously, as though he were a maître d' about to apologize for some terrible mistake.

"I was supposed to meet a friend but they never showed up," she said. "Aren't you going to make me a drink?"

Will slowly emerged from the shock of seeing Marla on his couch.

"Yes, yes, of course. Gin and tonic, with lime. I have ice." As he turned to go to the kitchen, he thought he glimpsed a slight expression of anxiety on Marla's face. This was hard for her, too, he thought, especially hard for her; she was in a strange person's house who hadn't been very clear about his intentions and who might even turn out to be unpleasant. Christ, he thought, we're both human beings. Why is it so hard to treat someone like a human being? Thinking these thoughts, he made the drinks, and as he returned to the living room, he realized he had talked himself out of even the slightest drop of sexual desire.

She was on the couch, her large shapely body folded in on itself, her skirt riding up over her thighs, which were covered with dark nylons. She looked anxious and helpless, and he found this attractive.

"Here," he said, handing her a drink.

He eyed the spot next to her on the couch and then opted for the relative safety of a chair next to it.

"So," he said.

"Well," said Marla. "Your place is very nice."

"I didn't get a chance to clean it up or anything. Usually when I have company..."

"No, it's nice. Besides, you didn't really have much warning." She gave Will a polite smile which was open to several thousand possible interpretations. She twirled her glass around, and the ice cubes clinked merrily. This gesture seemed very well-rehearsed, and for a moment she seemed completely composed, even powerful, like a television executive whose show was riding high on the charts.

Will gulped his drink. "It's weird to have you here," he said.

"Does it bother you?" she said. "I could just go."

"No, it doesn't bother me. It's just weird. I mean, I'm used to seeing you at work. It's like I only know you in that context."

"Well, I don't like that context very much. It's just so boring. You're sick of it, too."

"I arrived there sick of it, and it's been getting worse every day," he said. "It got a little better when you showed up, though."

She smiled a shy flattered smile, which made Will think about what she was like growing up, before she acquired the glowing feminine presence she now had. He wondered if her classmates made fun of her, if she had breasts when she was ten, if she was teased. She probably couldn't have been a cheerleader. He pictured her wearing one of those skimpy outfits, kicking her legs up and down out of time with the other cheerleaders, her pompons flying up and hitting her in the face.

"Were you a cheerleader?" he ventured. "You know, when you were in high school?"

"That's a strange question, Will. Why? Do I act like a cheerleader?"

"No, no, it's just, you know, Texas, high school football..."

"No, I wasn't a cheerleader," she sipped her drink. "I was in the marching band."

"Oh. Sort of a big jump from that to opera."

"My life is full of big jumps," she said.

"I'm glad you jumped to New York."

He leaned toward her, gulped his drink, and raked her body with his eyes.

Marla saw this and shifted her drink from one hand to the other. Her eyes narrowed but then opened, as if she had just remembered something.

"Well, it was nice having you as one of my early friends. And I do emphasize *early*, since you seem to have lost your enthusiasm for it lately."

"I have?" said Will defensively. "What do you mean?"

"What do I mean?" she said with some volume.

It dawned on Will that maybe she had come over to yell at him. He sat back in his chair.

"What do I mean?" she repeated. "I mean that one day you're buying me candy and hanging around and talking to me and the next day it's like I just offended your mother or something and you can hardly look at me."

"You didn't offend my mother," said Will, retreating into the literal as a defense.

"I know damn well I didn't offend your mother! So what did I do to make you so hostile all of a sudden?"

"I don't think the topic of my mother even came up."

Marla looked at him with exasperation. "Don't avoid the subject."

"What was the subject again? My mother?"

"Will!"

"Oh, was it *your* mother?"

"Will! Come on." Her voice softened a little and became small. "What did I do?"

"Well, you're here now, so what does it matter?" He stood up. "I need another drink. Can I get you one?"

She handed him her glass without saying anything.

When he returned he eyed the spot next to her on the couch but then returned to his chair.

"We don't even know each other," he said. "All I know about you is that you're from Austin and that you study opera and that you're going to be an opera diva or something. I don't even know much about opera. And you know even less about me. I wear a tie every day and work in a stupid office. You don't even know if I'm the president or some schlemiel in the back room."

"I'm sorry," said Marla, "but it's very obvious that you're a schlemiel in the back room."

He was amazed at how hurt he was by the statement of this simple fact, but he decided to ignore it.

"For all you know, I could be a psychotic killer. I could be a pervert. You know how it is, the guys walking around in ties and suits all day being polite, they have years of accumulated weirdness inside of them waiting to explode."

"Don't flatter yourself. There's not much killer in you. As for being a pervert..." She paused, as though it wasn't out of the question.

"I could be a poet, for all you know," he said, as if this was an even more horrifying prospect.

"Oh, could you?" she said facetiously.

Will stared at her face. The coffee stain birthmark throbbed just beneath her temple. He hadn't considered the possibility that she could be cruel, too, and its possibility interested him. He spoke calmly. "What do you think is going on with me, anyway? Do you think I *want* to be mean to you?"

"No, Will," she said, quite softly. "I think you're nice. You probably think you're less nice than you really are. You probably like the idea of it. But you *are* nice. I just don't know why you stopped being nice to *me*."

Her insight was true, and in telling the truth, she had exerted a form of power to which Will had no immediate response. He had made one tiny little experiment, a minor test, and the destruction was running rampant. It was out of his control. He tried to form a sentence but couldn't. And so—partly out of desire, partly because all other options had been exhausted—he lurched forward and pressed his lips against Marla's. They were warm and slippery with gin and lipstick, parted in surprise, soft and warm against his hard aggressive mouth.

She pulled back instinctively and pressed her hand against his chest, then relented a little, and his tongue found its way into her mouth for an awkward moment. Will remembered the confused look of concentration he had seen on her face that first day, with her full lips parted dumbly, and imagining that her face now had that same expression sent a surge of excitement through him. She pulled away just as he lunged forward in his desire, groping at her, and in one frantic moment, everything slipped away from him, including his drink, which landed right in the middle of her lap.

"Will!" she screamed.

"Oh shit," he said, referring as much to his unexpected gesture as to the stain that stretched from her waist nearly to her knees. Several ice cubes sat stranded on the grayish green fabric.

"Will!" she screamed again. "What's the matter with you!" She looked at him with wide incredulous eyes. "Go get me a towel, for Christ's sake!"

Will jumped off the couch and ran to the kitchen, returning with a clump of paper towels dangling from his outstretched arm like a bouquet of flowers.

"Here," he said. He watched as she attended to the wet spot with urgent, fussy energy. He stood over her for a moment and then, feeling silly standing there, started pacing the room in a circle.

"What's the matter with you?" said Marla again. "Don't they *train* men in New York? Does someone take you out for a walk on a leash when you get home from work?"

She seems upset, thought Will. "*God,*" he said sarcastically. "It's not that big a deal."

"And then you probably come home and eat dinner out of a bowl on the floor," she went on. Her head was down, and he thought he heard her voice crack. "You probably sleep on a pillow in a big wicker basket. You probably—"

"I didn't mean it," he said.

"I know just what you're thinking." Her voice lowered. She looked at him with narrow eyes. "Do you think this is news to me? You think you're a novelty? With your nervous stares, your little games."

"Oh shit," said Will, and he went into the bathroom, where he spent several minutes washing his face with cold water.

"I'm sorry about that," he said when he came out. "I'm just a little drunk."

"You're behaving awfully," she said. She was standing now, inspecting her skirt.

"You were the one who wanted to come over," he said, and immediately flinched because it sounded like a kid trying to get out of the blame for something. He didn't understand why he kept acting like a thirteen-year-old with this woman.

"Actually, I *accepted* your invitation. If you had said, 'Would you like to come over so I can maul you and spill my drink on you and then act unpleasantly?' I would have told you to fuck off."

"I'm sorry," he said.

"Is this how you normally relate to women?"

"No," he said. "I don't usually spill my drink on them." And then, "I must admit, you have a strange effect on me. I don't think I understand it."

They were standing several feet apart, facing each other, their bodies slightly taut, as if they were in a martial arts class and one of them was about to execute a takedown. Just then Will glanced over at the window and noticed he had neglected to pull the shades down. Across the alley stood another building, ridiculously close to his, its face a crossword puzzle of light and dark squares. He wondered if they had had an audience for the entire encounter, and he considered how the scene might have looked from a distance, viewed without sound, like a silent movie.

"Look," he said, "we've been performing. You like that, don't you? We've had our own little tragedy."

"More like a farce," she said.

He walked over to the window and cupped his eyes against it so he could see out better. When he first moved into the apartment, he had been horrified at how available other people's lives were to

him, but after a while he grew to like it. He marveled at apart-
ment buildings, at how lives could unfold in such proximity with-
out ever touching. Just then he could see a woman peeling
potatoes in her kitchen for what seemed like a large meal; next to
that, a couple curled up on their couch, bathed in the flickering
blue light of an unseen television.

"I don't know what you're doing," said Marla, "but I'm leav-
ing."

"Wait!" said Will. "I'm casing the joint. You have to know who
you're performing for. You're going to be a diva, right? A star. And
stars love to perform. I've never heard you sing."

Marla looked at him with an irritated expression and picked up
her purse. She took a few steps towards the door and turned to
him, inhaled, and let out a single burst of sound, a single high
note that elevated him off the floor for several seconds and then
dropped him, weak-kneed, back on his feet. She walked out with
an air of triumph, and let the door slam behind her. He stared at
it for a long time, half expecting it to open again. When it didn't,
he went and made himself another drink. He decided on the spur
of the moment to quit his job. He smiled weakly at the thought of
telling the vice president. He was quite shaken up. A stranger
looking in from across the alley could have seen it on his face.

Backswing

That's a cute-looking girl there
in the sports section.
A little flat-chested, but pretty.

The caption says: "Bubba Day follows through
on his way to victory in the Insurance Classic."
Wait a minute, is that a typo?

No, what I thought was a mistake
is really the truth. Her ponytail
is really his bicep on the backswing.

How come a cute-looking girl's
just an okay-looking guy, I ask myself?
Then I ask my wife

if she thinks he's cute
and she says, Yeah, but he wouldn't make
a good-looking woman.

Why's that? I ask. Because, she says,
it's easier for women to be cute-looking guys
than for guys to be good-looking women.

Why's that? I ask. Because, she says,
men make ugly women.
Okay, I say, put long blond hair on me.

Say, she says, what's your problem? I say,
For chrissakes can't you just do as I say?
She says, Okay, you're an ugly woman. I say, Ugly?

Look, she says, you've got a big nose, a beard,
and you're bald. But pretend I'm young, I say.
Look at my graduation picture. Whadda ya think?

She reads beneath it: "Good, better, best,
never take a rest until good is better and
better is best." So what happened? she asks.

Look, I say, I'm not joking. She says,
What's your problem, are you having a crisis?
Hell, no, I say, but I was turned on by a guy!

It's the woman in you, she winks. Look, I say,
can I get a straight answer to this? Well, she says,
if you were a woman, you'd have to learn to wait.

Who's talking about waiting? I say. You are,
she says. We're talking about double standards here.
I say, So what's your point? She says, You.

You think a cute-looking woman is just an okay-looking guy,
right? I say, Right but I'm getting a creepy feeling.
So, she says, look who's talking!

So, it's me? I say. Everything wrong in the world
comes down to me? She holds our baby up and says,
You think she's beautiful, right? And I say, Right.

So that shoots down your theory, she says. Theory?
I don't recall any theory. Did I say I have a theory?
Look, she says, has the picture changed or what?

And I say, No, yes, no, not really, and she says,
Are you going to make up your mind or what?
Then I squint at my wife who looks for all the world
like an Italian stud to me, and in my mind I pretend
the baby has a crew cut, and then I feel ambiguous or
ambivalent or whatever the hell it is.

Secrets of Water

Polymorphous perverse, dolphins of both genders prefer
sex-play with the human female.

1.
Water begins from a wound in the hillside, a tear in the
   clouds.
There's a tin cup no one cares has years of germs on its
   icy rim.

The water is sweeter than anything you will ever hold in
   your mouth.
And the spring doesn't start then stop. It's tireless and
   beneficent

yet nothing you do can make it love you in a different
   way—warmer
or more solid. The ocean held me under and I began to
   look around.

Everything looked like a world, not just a place to play. It
   was real,
separate from the air-world or the bonfire-world. I
   struggled, of course,

but noticed amazing things. How it must seem to a fish to
   go backwards
into the mouth of a great white shark, painlessly, as if
   the shark

were swallowing it whole. The sea was thick with light and
   people's legs
near shore were huge as pipelines and skinny as worms.
   The sun

was a memory, or the sun was a needle pushing gently
  through foam.
When you're drowning you cannot close your eyes for
  anything. You want

to look forever. There are your legs, frantic beneath you,
  and ten toes
licking the dark like little tongues. Your neck stretches
  out, chest

expands, everything about your body begins to bud and
  sing, hair
billowing gorgeously. Your debts don't matter, your hot
  flashes. Sand's

everywhere—crotch, cleavage, corners of your eyes. Such
  beauty,
and your fear so dazzling, benign. When they finally pull
  you out,

your lungs vomit sea into their beloved faces and they lean
  toward you,
like suns, asking are you okay. Their language breaks
  your heart.

2.
I keep thinking of my dead ex, Will, his circular life of
  Russian roulette,
that expulsion of singed air like breath from a slaughtered
  sea calf—

what comes to us in our meat and in our sewers—
  something pale
and ferocious rolling over and over in the shadows:
  chiaroscuro.

Black cars pass me on the Sprain Brook—a Toyota with
  four-wheel drive—

and I remember how Will took me to Fahnestock Park and
   we made love

in the back of his pickup. We were stretched across the
   Appalachian Trail
like islands and he was right—he'd never make it to forty.
   All this

fog around our bodies like the dreams of a thousand trout.
   We were wading
in the stream. We were hooking ourselves and throwing
   ourselves back in.

3.
The dolphin circles amiably. He has discovered my scent,
   my energy,
I can hear his sonar clicking like a child's toy, muffled and
   patient.

They say he can locate a metal plate in the brain, a
   pacemaker in the heart,
he's so bitingly intelligent the shark sighs and turns
   away. Still,

his penis brushing the back of my knee terrifies. I know he
   wants only
to play, to nudge and pull, sharing me with his curious
   mate, three

divine fishes easing through blue wake, skin like opals and
   quicksilver.
Will was slick with secrets. They hid beneath his skin,
   sloshing and feverish

as if his body were a cauldron or a dying star. He was a
   flawless lover,
coolest draft, generous as a flood, gifted with a global
   sensuality

that washed away continents and lives. He held me and his
    ribs were enormous,
impossible to hug all the way around, slippery as a cliff's
    wet face.

I thought this would feel religious—two species
    communing in a womb of salt.
Now six hundred pounds of mammal clock me as I
    backstroke to safety—

oxygen, earth, and fire pursued by lust and innocence. The
    ocean is opaque.
Bubbles float to the top and break like oracles from a
    lost treasure.

LEONARD NATHAN

Ah

Through an open window of late summer evening
a woman cries, Ah-ah-AH!

Neighbors pause, blush perhaps, then go on
with their homely chores, smiling to themselves.

What do you do with this—another's shameless,
lonely ecstasy? Or your own? I put

a tape of Mozart on to cover our confusion.

A Winter Affair

Love that arrives too late, untimely Eros
stumbles in after the fall has done
its worst, and winter fills the world with distance
and with snowfall far as hearts can feel.
Four crows creak in the cedar boughs,
symbols that signify themselves alone
since everything is what it only seems,
the least version of a possible self.
So Love limps to our fire, crouches, warms
his hands and tells a tale of transformation—
gray heads ablaze, sudden supernovas
of themselves. We shrug and sneer: "Old lies
to break old hearts," but then he unfurls his wings—
moth-eaten, ridiculous—and flies.

Graveyard Shift

By the light of the Last Days—
amber, a bit theatrical, a vacant lot light,

snowfall muffling the high-volt hum
transformers make zapping snowflakes

to kingdom come, somewhere off the interstate
outside Romeoville, Illinois—

the proof of which can be heard—
a ringing noise in the ear

louder and louder until it's a taxi horn
stuck & echoing off the bay doors—

by those who would only listen—
waking the attack dogs out back

for the octodecillionth time,
the guy, Mahmood, begging for wire cutters—

these backsliding days are numbered—
and, sadly, I have no wire cutters,

but I point him down the road
to the orange revolving ball—

Of the inferno, the grand enveloping fire—
where I think they'll have some wire cutters—

I can only say I hope you are ready—
The last few hours the worst,

mostly cops, a few drunks veering off the road—
to rise into the rapture—

a knocking sound, the furnace,
the day-shift guys clocking in—

whereafter, emptiness,
while the rest rise to greet the day.

Postcards and Joseph Cornell

The smart money spent the summer—
and left the poorer relatives agape,
and sent the change in ash and oak,
postmarked, *laughs galore in Smoky Mountains,*

& seashore where she sold her shells
& other things. The genre's born of envy:
If I were dead I'd write you still,
and come to you, tapping the ceiling fan.

You'd freeze despite the heat, stock-still,
and there I'd have you till you flicked the switch,
and that would be my message—*click*—
a matchbook, a toothpick, a lipstick laid

just so—to stay put, a brick in a box,
momento mori–wise—so a young man
shuffled the deck again, and a dead hand,
it seems, arranges things while we sleep.

Skin Trade

And then I said, That's what it means
to testify: to sit in the locked dark muttering
when you should be dead to the world. The muse
just shrugged and shaded his blue eyes. So naturally
I followed him down to his father's house
by the river, a converted factory in the old
industrial park: somewhere to sit
on threadbare cushions eating my words
and his promises, safe as milk
that dries the throat. If I had a home,
he'd be that unmade bed. He's my America
twisted in dirty sheets, my inspiration
for a sleepless night. No getting around that
white skin.
           He throws things out the window
he should keep; he collects things
he should feed to the river. He takes me
down. While there, I pick them up.

The river always does this to me:
gulls squawking and the smell of paper mills
upstream, air crowded with effluents
like riding the bus underwater. I'm spending nights
in the polluted current, teaching sunken bodies how
to swim. My feet always stay wet. Sometimes
I leave footprints the shape of blood; sometimes glass
flows through broken veins, and I glitter.
Every other step refers to white men
and their names. The spaces in between
are mine. *Back of the bus with you,*
nigger. They're turning warehouses
into condos, I'm selling everything

at clearance prices: here's a bronze star
for suffering quietly like a good
boy.
     River of salt, will I see my love again?
Cold viscous water holds its course even after
it's gone. Throw a face into it and you'll never look
again, throw a voice and you'll hear sobbing
all the way down. Narcissus, that's my flower
forced in January, black-eyed bells echoing
sluggish eddies. Who hit him first?

The muse has covered his face
with his hands. It's just a reflex
of the historical storm that sired him:
something to say, "The sun is beating down
too hard on my pith helmet, the oil slick
on the river's not my fault, when are you going
home?" What he doesn't want to see, he doesn't
see. In the sludge that drowns the river, rats
pick fights with the debris. He calls them all
by their first names, he's looking through his fingers
like a fence. They make good neighbors. His friends
make do with what they can. They drink beer
from sewer-colored bottles in the dry stream
bed, powdered milk of human kindness and evaporated
silt. They stay by the river till past
sunrise, crooning a lullaby
to help it to sleep. The words
of their drinking songs are scrawled on the ceiling,
Mene, mene, tekel, upharsin: a madrigal
for the millennium's end.
                   I'm counting
down the days in someone else's
unmade bed, let these things break
their hold on me. The world
would like to see me dead, another gone
black man. I'm still awake.

Eros in His Striped Blue Shirt

and green plaid shorts goes strolling
through Juneau Park at eight o'clock
with only a hooded yellow windbreaker
for protection, trawling the bushes after work

while tugboats crawl the dark freshwater
outlook. Mist coming in not even from a sea, rain
later in the evening from Lake Michigan, a promise
like *wait till your father gets home.* The air

is full of fog and botched seductions, reluctance
of early summer to arrive. It's fifty-five degrees
in June, the bodies can barely be made out
leaning on picnic tables under trees or

set sentinel like statues along the paths (the founder
corrodes quietly on his pedestal, inscription
effaced under FAGGOTS GO HOME). Lips
touched to a public fountain for a passerby

shape clouded breath into a *who-goes-there?,* into a
friend-or-foe?, eyes catching eyes like hooks
cast in a shallow tide. Night pouring in like water
into a lock, the rusted freighter lowered level

to level, banks of the cement canal
on either side, but miles from any dock.

SUZANNE PAOLA

Conception

From a sparse
handful of seed
comes summer—

Corn and convolvulus. Scatter
of color on the mountainside,
near snow.

Gone, we want to say, of some longing
in the slim afternoon—

Though poppies collapse to soft flesh
at a touch, heather
tolls its little bells...
        •
A bee, trapped
between windowpanes.
Its three lives
clearly visible—

The past (a meadow)

there, on one side.
The future it wings toward
(bowl of old plums)
opposite,

beyond glass—

Itself at the median point, where *been*
and *will be* strut
and freeze.

So this is the present, this small clear room...
•

There were stars, of course,
in some sort of arrangement.
An inch of drink
in the glass. Worn clothes.

A man and a woman lay down together
& three arose.

Sakti

Sakti: a feminine power in Hindu thought—
creative, perhaps destructive

In my small
niece's room, the walls
throb pink: pink tights
lie, thrown
on a flowered spread. Rose frills, mauve,
& pearl—
   Girl
colors, blended of blood & milk.
A sprawled doll, & through the window
fat, voluptuous clouds above the sea.

The forms of the feminine are everywhere—
•
Of course we remember:
The first, slow knowledge—that of two bodies, we have the
 wrong one.
So we cover our breasts before they even are breasts
as if shame lies in the intent, nature's drive toward the female.
Because breasts *will* emerge, into small domed bandages,
the menses will come, dark drool at the lips.
Vulva will spread, the small field grow.
•
What's better than a woman? the poster says.
Beer—it stays wet
& the container's still worth something after use.
I think about this, in the milky moonlight of New Orleans,
how hard it is to turn, consciously, to the feminine.
How otherwise we die, as Diderot said, at fifteen
into symbol, statuary in the male garden.
Where we lose what we have, the soft fluid spreading of the
 woman,

our voids places of abundance, our emptiness,
always, possibility.
•

Moonlight & the feminine—
We're ruled, myths tell us, by her hag-lined,
preternatural face...
Twin-caverned, eyed
like a child, but earless, mouthless, deaf
   goddess, goddess of the mimed prayer—
Who draws the blood
from our wombs as she draws the oceans
slapping & spittling the shoreline,
as she draws waters
even in the smallest cells...
Deep in our bodies, floodtide & neaptide, & ocean's beat
   in our ears—

Dark & ugly, she rocks us
like an old witch in a fairy tale,
saving us from stillness, saving us from rest.
•

To call the lips of the vagina petals
To call the menses an essence of the moon
Would be to miss the essential point: the thisness of the female.
That we *are* flesh & blood: chapped flesh & black blood
& from these emerge
the improbable, the carnal world—

our bodies geniuses
of dust, & its secret motes
moving in silent passion with the moon.

NICOLE COOLEY

Confession

The Roosevelt Mineral Baths

Do you believe the proof is not in the body?
In the name of the Father, Son and Holy Ghost,
John walks among the olive trees by the river,

looking for the women who will let him touch
their faces with his hands. At night in the park
I unwind the scarf from my hair, preparing to enter

the water. I yield to the stone tub as if I were giving
myself up for sleep. My body floats like a lozenge
in yellow light. My body has nothing to do with the world.

I want to believe in the promises of grace. Father, I want
to reach you. In the room full of saltwater Alice cannot find
the path to the shore. She knows that to pass through

to the garden is hopeless and remembers the bathing machines
for girls by the sea and his gift to her: the straw hat spinning
over the sand. There are no other girls, no use looking for God

or the Reverend or another way to become small for the door.
We are the brides confessing our sins to the one
who could love us, who could lead us down with him

to the other world. By the waters of baptism we want
to be buried with Christ in his death. The punishment is not
drowning but another terror—the body transfixed

in water, held still in the bath. In the garden Easter lilies nod
on their stems, the crystal fountain gleams in the sun.
The body fails to answer. The body fails again and again.

Tonight, the water will not take us to the world
every story promises, the world of forgiveness below
the sulfur water, the lake of a girl's sorrow, the pool of tears.

Reenactment

We squat in the sun, in black dirt
abraded from the mountain.
You prick my arm with a thorn. "Does it hurt?"
It does hurt. We're playing nurse and mother
getting her abortion. You draw out
all my blood, then with invisible gauze
from your imaginary white enamel tray
bandage my sore arm.

In her small vacation room, your mother
coils around her cramps, easing now.
Months before she was born, a doctor
offered to take her from me. I said "No."

You don't understand absence, and I myself
have forgotten the urgency for shelter,
how a bed and dresser in a small room,
a single light bulb, do comfort
our sleeping and waking and turning.

Confinement

Catherina Schrader, midwife,
nearly an apparition in mists rising
from the Wadden Zee,
follows a stranger to his boggy farm.

The man is afraid of his wife,
her cries, her twisted face.
Who knows what may enter a woman
and flourish there?

There have been stories—monsters
with fingers and toes grown together
like pigs' feet or skin scaled as a fish's
or no face at all or a brain
growing outside of its head—a child alien
as any gift from the supernatural.

Vrouw Schrader worries, the child seems so still.
Sometimes the strongest longing is to die,
to turn from welcoming hands and burrow
deep into the plush cave, back to the mother heart.
Vrouw Schrader has made a pact with life
and drags the obstinate child into it.

Bloody. Hungry. Afraid.

Sighting the Whale

The mother kneels beside her grieving child,
grieving because the whale has not come,
because the whales are elsewhere, not heaving

clear of the water where child
and mother can see them. In the brilliant light
of a day at sea, the child whimpers.

Her own small sea ebbs and rolls until
she spews an orange tide—tomato pulp,
peppers, sausage chunks from last night's pizza.

She sleeps, cleansed. Radioed that the whale is near,
we speed to a gigantic, scarred, half-sick
elephant's trunk of a thing bulging

from the sea, barnacles crusted
to his black hide like orange wounds.
The young mother vomits quietly

into her handkerchief, turning it over
and over, liquid and warm in her palm,
her other hand soothing the sleeping child.

Dinner in the Fall

Partially green leaves are falling
on Camille's Italian restaurant
where grapes tint our lips, and the linens
are more inviting than our bed.
Our eyes shine like the blue
glaze on our plates. Heat
radiates through the shale of my spine
now suddenly recalling
the black bitter chill of deep sea
as if my body doesn't know how
to assimilate the taste
of calamari. Your infatuation
blooms in this moment
without root or rain. A breeze
plays your hair like a lyre, octaves
I can't hear. Everywhere
I look, a clean glass
sparkles in someone's hand.
If only we could be living
our afterlives now
without climax, regret or redemption,
knowing what to say to each other.
We laugh, as if we had not flung back
the promise of a child and now
here you are, your dark curly hair
playing unknown melodies,
your cheeks pink as a fisherman's
returning from the sea.

Phoenix

It was the wrong place to look
for resurrection. Memorial Day,
one hundred four degrees Fahrenheit.
Cloudless sky. Square parking lots
surrounding new motels. Always more
loss required, always. And after,
feeble gestures to shape what
remains into a marvelous bird.

It would have been fine with me
to know only enough of grief to
bear a wren or a sparrow. A tiny
passing song from a little mound
of soot. *No, no,* says your heart
make a peregrine falcon, a red-
tail hawk. Hoard loss until
you hear the sweep of its wings.

I was told go to the city where
firebirds rush through the air
of burnt light, where imported palm
trees slump in the sand. What rises
is not a bird or the soul provided
relief, but scents of fast-food
burger grease, cod and halibut
frying at the Long John Silver's.

It's not your fault your name intimates
magic. To walk these streets is
to walk on coals. I was without her.
I needed someplace to take my ashes.

The Gust

In the mind
there comes a moment
when shadows fall back   like men
from a gust of something,
when the brain is light
as a fly on your wrist—

and in the jeweled eyes of that fly
you see your own six-legged self
white-shoed, dancing,
being on parade—
the gold tuba grown from your lips:
Um-pah-dah   cha-cha   huuh!

Meet me there.

Ten Miles an Hour

The weird thing about the place was the speed of light—
eight, nine miles an hour, tops. Isweartagod!
It was beautiful, though, the way it felt slowing over you
like a balmy breeze—light slow enough to catch in a,
in a cup, light you could smear on a slice of bread
like jam, light you could rub into your hair like Sulphur 8.

And there were other things. For example,
just about everybody but little kids could outrun it—
something we never consider here with the photons
doin' 186,000 miles a second. So, say you saw
some skinhead mothafucka with a swastika on his cheek.
You could holla, *Hey, you pea-brained, goose-steppin',*
kitty-litter suckin', sick-ass Nazi, then take off.
Once you hit ten miles per hour you would disappear
till you broke back to a trot. That's the beauty
of slow light—no muss, no fuss:
now you see a brother—now you don't.

Anyway, this is how it really went. First,
I should say there were no cars for obvious reasons,
and getting to this spot is a long haul on foot:
down this long alley, over three rocky hills,
gotta wade through this one muddy river,
and there's a forest somewhere, dark and spooky—
made me feel like Red Riding Hood.
So, when I arrive I'm tired and my sneaks are soggy—
like I'm wearing wet biscuits on my feet. Everything
looks blurry—like, like when you move a camera
just as you snap the shot.

Pretty soon, though, I notice that nobody's poor   nobody,
and I come to this park and there's a sister
straddlin' this Hawaiian dude who's sitting on a bench.

Her skirt's hiked up, she got them big legs shinin'
and I mean they're gettin' it, gettin' it good
to the last drop   right there. And it wasn't about
showin' off. They coulda been hid way away somewhere,
two good people takin' care of business, you know—
T-C'in' on the B like it wasn't no helluva big thing.

And there was this bunch of reddish-gold birds—
looked like pigeons—and all these kinky-haired kids
chasing them across the grass with painted leaves,
and together they made a noise like someone   someone
munching Cracker Jacks near a microphone.

So, I just start dancin'—no music but that—I just
take off my clothes and start wavin' my arms and hoppin'.
I'm steady shakin' my yams, my jammy's jingle-jumpin',
and pretty soon it's me and two other brothers   then,
these Turkish cats fall in on congas   and this
Jewish honey and her extremely fine friend from Laos—
Isweartagod! And *then*   this Ethiopian mamasita, a real
killer-diller, busts in the circle wit' this Mexican,
Mississippi Masala–lookin' girl, and I turn
to this Eastern Bloc brother named Gustav and holla,
*Oh no, say it ain't so—don' NObody need to have
no BODY like that!* So we grab our gear, get dressed,
and follow them to this place called Logan's: black tables,
big sofas, soft single chairs covered in lazuli blue.

Somebody hits the dimmers. I ride the light over slow, like,
like a loose clump of new weather, and open my mouth
to the first words that gang up inside my teeth: *Excuse me,
ladies, but my blood's all tied in a knot, and I
was wondering if you might help me get it undone.*
Ethiopia nudges Mexico and asks me if the knot in question
might require both of them. No lie!
But I don't wanna fade on Gustav; I nod his way. Like smoke,
his smile floats over. So, she closes her eyes and I see
that her friend's hand has wandered under her dress,

lingering there with small, graceful undulations. I'm
diggin' it, but I'm not sure what it means. So,
I shrug and get ready to step back when Mexico says,
Taste this, holding up two wet fingers.

Well, what would you have done? Been scared
and said, *Um, no thanks—I'm driving*. Man,
I could spend my life tryin' to name that flavor.
Anyway, Alandra (that's her name), gets up with them legs
that go *all* the way down, and I can feel some story
starting to untell, my body calling *open-says-a-me*
to all its magic doors. Next thing I know,
we're dancing to this oldie slow jam:

> *I'm an ever-rolling wheel*
> *without a destination real*
> *I'm an ever-spinning top*
> *going around   till I drop*

      You know that moment when two bodies find out
how they fit together, as though one torso
is hinged to the other, as though you're both
perfectly matched pieces in some sweet, nobody-ever-
told-you-about-it, sho-nuff forever and always jigsaw—
me and Alandra are falling into place.

> *You got me going in circles*

      Later, we step outside. It's sundown.
You could see the last puddles of sunlight
drying up, going dark, and the streetlamps
slowly throwing their lazy glow like Rapunzel
rolling down her three stories of hair.

I mean, up until just now, I thought I might still have been
standing somewhere in America, but the night held no threat,
and across the road, I remember, two men resting in each
    other's arms.

And her kiss, the taste of her mouth opening like a sleepy
    carnival
into mine, and Gustav and Genet against the magnolia,
    fucking
like dancing, like doing some delicious naked salsa,

my lungs squeezing more and more oxygen into my blood,
    my brain
bright orange like a tropical fish, Alandra bringing me
into her skin, holding on, taking me up like some kind of
origami bird she could balance on her lips.

And the not-out moon, the sharp whelming of what
is never seen   and the voice coming all undone,
but for the one long syllable, and Isweartagod!

There is a place not all that far from here
where glad drums whistle
all the answers to the riddles of bone.

Say whatchuwanna, but inside my hand
there is a sound and inside that sound
there is a city and inside that city
it is early—with you already awake,

your hand like mine, like a rooster,
throwing itself open, loud, each finger
a street vendor crowing the first light
free—along with all the big, blue-apple muffins,
the crowded carts of cantaloupe, and the T-shirts

and the clear castle of air,
and everything else   everything

Playing Catch

for Hermann Michaeli

On the day the balls disappeared, men playing soccer
suddenly looked like crazy people chasing invisible
rabbits through the short grass. Men playing baseball
became more clearly what they'd always been: bored
teenagers waiting around for something to happen.

Spectators, at home and in the stands, believed
they were being jerked around by a player
conspiracy, that this was the first whimper
of another strike that would cancel all the fun.

On the day the balls disappeared, the sun did not
smear its way up above the dew-damp rooftops as if *this*
were a day to keep your finger on. And if all the umps and refs
overslept that morning, it only meant they were a little extra
tired of instant replay highlighting their best mistakes.

In fact, it was a good Saturday: sunlight the color of a canary—
everybody was outside! I remember one woman in particular,
alone in the schoolyard practicing lay-ups. Each time
she left the ground she balanced the basketball like
a breakable thing, then let it slip off her long
white fingers toward the rim.

It had been August for more than a month and, as usual,
the televisions were jam-packed with sports: preseason
football, golf, baseball, soccer, some rugby . . . If you didn't
know better watching TV could make you think the world
was really just a million fields separated by a few
rivers and roads—that life was, in essence, a chance
to love one of the many artificial spheres.

I guess they went all at once or, at least, within
the same fifteen minutes. I had been watching the U.S.
Open Tennis Championships when Pete Sampras, ready
to serve, gestured to the ball boy who quickly
pointed at the other and shrugged, hoping not
to be blamed. People in the stadium began whistling
and stomping their feet. I went to the fridge
and grabbed a plum.

                  But I remember noticing
a boy and his sister across the street playing catch
in the yard half-framed by my kitchen window.
He had a new red glove. She was a lefty and
brown as coffee, and, just to show off, she whipped
the throw just above his reach.
                      A moment later
he yelled, *I can't find it—I don't see it—*
it ain't out here! She thought he just wanted *her*
to go get it, just to get on her nerves. She thought
he was just kidding around.

Scavenger Bird

Finding things had always been her greatest pleasure. She was not systematic, not one of the ones who bought the local paper and mapped out a route between all of Saturday's yard sales. What she loved was driving down the road and coming upon the sign—a rough paper bag tacked to a telephone pole, or a neatly lettered cardboard square stapled to a piece of wood: Garage, White Elephant, Rummage, Yard, Moving, Estate, Porch, Tag Sale. This, or even better, a trash heap with something old, something wooden and only slightly broken, leaning up against the bags or not quite buried among their fat, green shapes.

She found it difficult not to slow down on garbage day, found it impossible not to stop when she saw a sign, even if she had already been to a few sales that morning. Just for a second, she would tell herself. One sign would lead to another, and another, down side streets or dirt roads. She would follow the skewed arrows until suddenly, like a guest who had come from far away, she'd find herself in front of the house.

She loved that moment, looking up and seeing a big brick colonial, or a modern A-frame, or a tumbledown farmhouse with no front steps. Sometimes a little prefab ranch house with plastic deer in the yard would yield an intricate beaded purse from the twenties, or a faded handmade quilt with tiny black ants stitched around the flowered squares. In some ways, the less she liked the owner's taste, the more chance she had of finding good stuff, since only things considered junk by their owners would be sold for pennies on the front lawn.

If she had time, she sometimes even lingered at a bad sale. People put amazing things out, put garbage, and this fascinated her as well, so that she looked at broken, burned kettles or stained baby clothes, old brassieres and potty chairs, half-filled bottles of hand lotion, boxes of unidentifiable scraps of metal. Once she saw a Campbell's soup can—not old, certainly not antique. Cream of

Mushroom, rinsed clean and put out on the table like a Warhol piece. Not a joke, she was pretty sure, unless the dour women behind the table had the driest and most hidden sense of humor she had even seen. Days when she was in a rush, she did a rapid, back-and-forth inventory with her eyes and hands, patting, brushing, rifling, the way her grandmother must have when she went to the open market in Russia as a girl.

Sometimes she would look down and spot a cobalt-blue salt shaker with a tarnished silver-plate casing, or a battered wooden shelf, or a painted tin box with buttons inside—and buried beneath the buttons, a pin marked Secret Seven, and small, sharp tools she could not name. Her throat would catch then, would actually get clogged with pleasure, and her hands would itch to polish and refinish, to rub oil in circles on the wood and touch up the metal with ceramic paint.

This habit of hers—this bargain-hunting, poking-about obsession—was not shared by her boyfriend, Tom, who slept on a secondhand futon and kept his books in cardboard boxes. He had, in his studio apartment, exactly as many things as he needed: maybe three plates, two mugs, two blankets, one table, a coffee maker, two chairs, one desk, plus a few odds and ends that previous tenants had left shoved back on the kitchen shelves. This bothered her in a number of ways. First, she itched to fill up his place—to rummage through the backs of his cupboards, see what she could find, and then begin to accumulate, use wall space, organize books. Then that impulse irked her; it made their roles seem so stereotyped, as if, in a cartoon of the two of them, she would wear an apron, grasp furniture polish in one hand and an old shelf in the other, while he would hold a cigarette and book.

In fact, she read, too; they had met at the bookstore where they worked, both of them the same age and vaguely thinking of graduate school. She had noticed him her first day there because of his beauty—blond and chiseled, long-legged, long-haired, terribly careless, the kind of man she would have yearned for in high school, watched and obsessed over and never approached.

This time she did approach. They spent hours together working in the bookstore, of course, but it was she who invited him first for coffee; then, in a phone call so difficult to make that she had to drink nearly a bottle of wine before she could do it, out to dinner. She wasn't sure why she found the courage to invite him finally, except that she was tired of looking at men and hardly ever touching them, and something about him (he seemed very alone and half-unaware of his own beauty) made her brave.

At dinner they drank more wine, talked about books. She had been surprised that he smoked; he looked more like a hippie, someone who ate health food, and then she remembered his constant brief absences from work and realized he'd been popping outside for a cigarette. She did not like it when he started to smoke in the restaurant—it jarred with her image of him—but in other ways he seemed perfect: smart, political, offbeat. Sometime late in the evening, back in her apartment, she touched his blond hair. They were drunk. A heavy lock was hanging over his eye, and she reached over and smoothed it back, which was very unlike her, to make the first move. It worked; it was a revelation to her, that she did not have to wait, that she could lift her hand and make one tiny, stupid little move, and he would fall almost helplessly into her arms.

He loved sex. That was one of the confusing things about him. He was remote in a way; he could be distant and judgmental, but he loved sex, and not just sex but touching, proximity—a leg, an arm, a toe linked with hers. He loved the curve of her hip, the back of her knee, her thick eyebrows. And he told her so, almost as if his own reaction had taken him by surprise, so that he seemed, in those moments, not the man who tossed his hair back in a gesture arrogant enough to belong to a rock star, not the almost surly, ironic bookstore clerk, but something else. He reminded her then of the sea anemones she had seen on the rocks in Olympia National Park. They were gray, thick-skinned, covered with barnacles, but on some impulse, one of them would breathe open, and you'd see its insides, wet and smooth like the wall of a mouth, tulip pink or a nearly fluorescent green.

They had been together for a bit over a year the day she found the desk. It was not an easy relationship; several times they had almost broken up. She needed more reassurance than he wanted to give and got irritated with herself for it; and he (what was his story? She wasn't at all sure), he fell into moods so dark and long and private that she could only watch from a distance, moving from bemusement to irritation and frustration and, finally, suppressed anger and then bemusement again, since his moods would vanish without warning, and he would seek, almost desperately, her touch.

But the day she found the desk, things had been going all right. It was early fall. They had talked, even, about living together soon. She, of course, had brought it up. She had wanted him to but had known he never would; finally she had figured what the hell. He did not say no. He nodded and said they should think about it. She had been thinking about it, for much longer than she would ever admit to him. Sometimes, in her thoughts, they were in bed or shopping at the farmer's market, or sitting reading, each in a big old chair, or at opposite ends of the couch with their feet entwined. Sometimes they were cooking, cutting up red and yellow peppers, sautéeing garlic, or kneeling on an imagined screen porch tearing mint leaves from stems.

Other times, her mind grew smaller and she couldn't see these things as well. He didn't like to cook, she would realize. He didn't, in fact, like furniture, or vegetables. He liked his apartment to be filled with boxes so that it always looked like moving day. One day she borrowed a book from him and noticed how the pages smelled like stale smoke. She did not let him smoke in her apartment, but if they lived together, she would have to. And if they broke up, her things would smell of his smoke, a lingering, persistent smell, and she would have to begin again.

She found an old school desk on the street. She was on her way home from work and saw it in someone's trash heap, by a big white house with a slate mansard roof, the kind of house an old widow probably lived in, with a car in excellent repair parked neatly in its drive. She pulled over, got out. It was an old, small, elegant child's desk with rusted wrought iron legs and a dark wood top coated with grime. She put it in the back of her car, and when she got to her street, she parked and carried it to her apartment, hardly believing her good luck. By the time she got it up the stairs, her white shirt was smudged dark gray and deep crayony orange from the grime and rust.

At home she bathed the desk, washing off layer after layer of dirt until she reached its scarred, dark wood. She knelt in her bathroom, her jeans wet and smeared with dirt, her fingertips clean and wrinkled from the water. It was not until she was rubbing the desk down with Murphy's Oil Soap, watching its colors deepen to mahogany, that she saw the swastika carved neatly in its corner.

"Shit," she said.

She had never seen one, not up close, not unmediated by a picture, a textbook, or a movie. She had grown up a non-practicing Jew in a small New England town full of Christians. Once or twice she had been asked by her teachers to explain Hanukkah, and a few times she had been called Jewgirl by some creepy boy, but among all the graffiti on desks in her years at school, she had never seen a swastika. Now here one was, right in her bathroom, spiked and symmetrical, written on her find like "Mary + Kenny" or "Fuck Physics" or "True Love Always."

For a moment she backed up from the desk, which she had already grown to love, and saw it as something alien, hostile. It could have that look; its legs were rusted, its feet commanding and thick. Its mouth was gaping, its ink hole as dark as an eye poked out, a place to lose things. She pictured a tough, angry, anti-Semitic little boy in the early nineteen-forties taking out a penknife when his teacher's back was turned, making one line, waiting for the teacher's back to turn again, making the next line. A tough guy, or maybe a quiet, hidden type, a careful carver, probably good at geometry, all the edges equally spaced out and straight. *Asshole,* she thought, and in her mind she slapped him hard across his pudgy, stunned, old-fashioned face. Or maybe it was more recent; it wouldn't surprise her in this Vermont college town, which fancied itself progressive but did not like outsiders. She always seemed to find herself living in places where there were no Jews.

But then she looked at the desk again, and its wood was gleaming, and the swastika looked smaller, tucked up in the corner. The desk was, after all, a find, just waiting for her by the side of the road. If this boy had sat at it with his angry, his twisted little mind, so had hundreds of other kids, or maybe he hadn't even know what a swastika was, had just been imitating, or maybe it was a prewar carving. She had read somewhere that before Hitler took the swastika over and bent its edges, the same sign signified (in India, or was it Japan?) something like eternal life. In any event, she had already decided, as she was driving home, where the desk would go—by the bay windows at the front of her apartment, with a cactus on it, and her old wooden flying shuttle, and the box that flipped inside out and turned into a stand covered with crooked, numbered hooks.

She hardly thought about what she did next; she acted as if she had been issued a command, though she could not have said by whom. She went into the kitchen and got a sharp paring knife, rubbed the desk down with a cloth to make sure it was dry. Then, kneeling again, the overhead light on, she filled in the gaps on the symbol, made each line connect with another until there was not a swastika before her, but a neat four-squared grid. It still did not look right, her lines too raw and new, so she took a bottle of India ink and rubbed a little over the cuts, which ran in black until they looked like the old ones. Then she wiped the surface down with oil. It had worked; you could never tell.

She would still have to get rust remover and repaint the legs black, but that could wait. She brought the desk into the main room of the apartment, pushed a trunk aside, and put the desk in its place. She covered it with its intended objects, backed up from it, and stared. It looked—she was quite sure—as if it belonged there. She put on some jazz and lay down to take a nap.

He half woke her with his key turning, then woke her more with his hands sliding up her shirt. Sometimes he arrived like this, wordless and hungry. She loved that, the way they could dispense with all formality, all hellos, and simply greet each other with fingertips. They played for a while, nuzzling, half napping. Then he started to get up, to pee probably; he peed more often than any man she had ever met.

She hesitated, but then the words came out. "Look what I got."

She did not always show him her finds. He was not, for one, particularly interested, and it depressed her to hear his fake, conversational attempts to appreciate what she had brought home. But it went deeper than that, for on some level she felt he disapproved, found her too acquisitive, too much the consumer, he who went to Democratic Socialists of America meetings and never bought anything but books. Or perhaps it was her own dis-comfort with her quest for objects, the fact that she knew it to be close to an addiction. She could, if she needed to, drive right by, but her hands would itch and her stomach contract with the grim, thudding feeling of having just lost a perfect thing.

Still, at times something made her want to show him—pride and pleasure, partly, in what she had found, but partly a desire to force herself out into the open, to admit her glee and see if he would still want her.

"The school desk," she said. "By the front window."

"Hold on. I'm bursting."

She lay there listening to the familiar splash of his pee, then the flush.

"By the window," she repeated when he came back in.

He zipped as he walked, went over to the desk, ran a finger on its edge.

"Huh. Where'd you find that?"

"On the street, in someone's garbage pile."

"Yeah? I guess they were cleaning out their attic."

"It's pretty old. It has an inkwell, look. Behind the plant."

He peered, nodded, and returned to her bed.

"My magpie," he said. "My scavenger bird." He kissed her neck and started to unbutton her shirt. She pictured herself then as a blackbird with a sharp, yellow beak, enfolding a pale, blond man in the iridescence of her wings. Was that what a magpie looked like? She knew they were related to crows. She wasn't sure she liked him calling her that, though he had been doing it since he first saw her drag something home off the street. Magpies, of course, collected bright metal objects and brought them to their nests. That was fine with her, but she had read in a bird guide at the bookstore that they killed other birds' babies and ate their eggs, and she was quite sure they had some old, unfriendly association with Jews.

"Magpies don't wear shirts," he said, and she kissed his palm to stop him from unbuttoning her. That was when she told him, almost knowing she was asking for trouble, that his reaction would be complicated, though she could not have predicted exactly how.

"It had a swastika on it," she said.

"What?"

"The desk had a swastika carved on the top, in the corner."

"Really." He sat up. "Let me see."

"It's not there anymore. I got rid of it."

He turned to look at her. "How'd you do that?"

"I carved it into a grid."

He stood and walked over to the desk, lifted first the cactus, then the flying shuttle, until he found the etched black squares. He came back to the bed and sat leaning on the wall.

"That's sort of a weird thing to do, don't you think?"

"Why?"

"To turn a swastika into a windowpane, or whatever. It's still a swastika, underneath."

"Well, I'd rather not have it in my apartment."

"But you do." His voice was agitated, and she, too, suddenly felt panicked and unsure. "You do have it here," he said. "I hate that about Americans. It's not in your apartment if you color in the lines so you can't see it?"

"Americans?" She drew her knees to her chest, zipped her jeans, which he had undone. "You hate that about Americans? Aren't you overgeneralizing a little? Who are you, for example?"

"Okay," he said. "Okay, fair. Your call." He sometimes used terms like this, as if they were in a law court or a sports field; he had, in fact, been an obsessive athlete, a soccer player, before he discovered books. "Not Americans, then, but upper-class, privileged, nostalgic Americans, the kind who buy old washboards because they think they're cute."

"What do you mean?"

"Oh, come on, Sarah," he said. "The whole antique thing. I mean, I don't want to criticize you, and I guess I'd rather be surrounded by your stuff than by, I don't know, steel and chrome, but it's this kind of false nostalgia. I mean, some lady buys a washboard because it has old writing on it and she thinks it'll perk up her mantelpiece, but shit, someone broke their back using that washboard, and then they ditched it for a washing machine the second they could—if they could afford to."

He's right, she thought. The words always came to him so easily.

And yet then she was not so sure. She hated, for one, the way he used the word "lady." Why couldn't the washboard have been bought by a man, or at least a woman?

"Can't someone buy a washboard," she said, "because he wants to understand its history, not nostalgically—okay, maybe a little nostalgically—but mostly because he wants to touch stuff other people—in the past, you know—have touched? It's like a continuity or something..."

She couldn't explain what she meant, even though it was, in a way, so simple. She loved imagining all the fingers that had fingered the things she touched, all the faces that had looked at them, the dust that had sprinkled them, the light that had touched them, the conversations they had witnessed. But he did have a point. She had bought that wooden flying shuttle, after all, and though she had read about millworkers in college—the long hours, the accidents, the racket of the power looms—how much did she really think about it? She had wanted the shuttle because it was shaped like two bows facing each other and made of a rich, dark, oily wood, with a tight skein of black yarn in its center and gleaming metal tips on each end.

"Okay," he said, "then if an object carries history, you can't just whoosh it away. Someone carved a swastika on that desk. It's part of its history."

Yes, she thought, and was surprised at how strongly the thought presented itself to her: Part of its history, but not part of yours.

He was of old Norwegian-American stock. His family, on both sides, had been farming in the Midwest for over a hundred years, but by the time they got to him, they had prospered and left the land. One grandfather had been a businessman, the other a judge; his father was a lawyer, like hers, though not, in fact, she imagined, like hers at all. She had never met his family, but she had seen pictures, and they all looked like him, with long bones and thick, dirty-blond hair. She lusted after this sort of man. She did not know why. Perhaps it was some twisted form of self-hatred, or because they looked the opposite of her father, or maybe it was just that she grew up in a town filled with long-legged blond boys who played soccer and skied, and she yearned for them through her adolescence because they did not seem to yearn for her. When she got a little older, her taste changed, but just a bit. She liked the Waspy boys turned rebels, the ones who grew their hair and went to demonstrations, who left their thrones of privilege to work in food banks or even just bookstores. She wanted a political boyfriend, so why did she feel so angry now, so invaded, as if he were poking at her with a stick?

"Jesus," she said. "It's a desk. It's something I found on the street. You think I should have left that thing on it, kept it like that?"

"I would have."

"You wouldn't have taken it."

You wouldn't have seen it, she was thinking. He worked more hours at the bookstore than she did, and when he wasn't there, or with her, he read—as he walked, as he sat on buses.

"Probably not, but if I had, I wouldn't have turned a swastika into a tick-tack-toe game."

She turned away from him.

"What?" he said. "I'm just wondering why you did it. I wouldn't have done that."

"You," she said, "don't know what it feels like to look at one of those things from my perspective, so I wish you'd stop announcing what you'd do."

He knew she was Jewish, but they hardly ever discussed it, just as it hardly ever presented itself as a major fact in her life. It was more a subtle backdrop, a feeling of always being a bit outside. Now she heard herself speak and was troubled to realize that she was not sure she meant everything she said. After all, she had reacted to the swastika when she first saw it in the bathroom, but it had not horrified her, not the way it perhaps should have. She had wanted the desk more, wasn't that it? She had found it and wanted it in her house, and changed it with a few rapid strokes so it could stay.

"You mean because you're Jewish," he said.

She nodded.

"Well, yeah, you're right, I'm not Jewish, but that doesn't mean it doesn't affect me. I've read about it, for Christ's sake, and tried to understand."

"It's a desk," she said. "Some kid probably carved that thing without even knowing what it meant. Not everyone is as miraculously educated and conscious as you."

"So first," he laughed, "it means more to you because you're Jewish, and then it means nothing at all because whoever carved it didn't know shit. You're quite a contradiction."

Was she quite a contradiction? She guessed she was. She knew the Lord's Prayer from going to church with her friends on Christmas Eve, and *Baruch Atah Adonai* from her family's perfunctory Hanukkah celebrations. She had probably spent more time in churches than in synagogues, but as a girl, before her grandfather died, she had listened to him chant at Passover (in Russia, his father had been a rabbi), and found herself oddly moved and fascinated by the plate in the middle of the table. First of all, it had compartments and was filled with things, and then the things themselves were so strange: the gnarled bone she wanted to suck on, the hot pink clump of horseradish, the cloudy, ashen egg.

Her grandparents on one side had died before she was born. The other set—now just her grandmother—lived in Co-op City in the Bronx, where there were as many people in one building as in her entire town, her father said. It had always felt like a different world there, one she was not sure of. Her father had gotten his law degree, married her mother, who was from Queens. They moved to a small town and had three girls. But the Bronx was where he had begun, in a building now gutted and burned out. Her parents' furniture was Scandinavian and sleek, but her grandparents had heavy, old furniture in golds and maroons. Her grandmother kept plastic on the pleated lampshades and the arms of the couch and put out fake candied oranges in a cut glass dish. The apartment was overheated, cramped, with knickknacks on the windowsills and shelves. They ate dinner on tin card tables painted with flowers, and she was not allowed to have milk with meat, or help herself to dishes, or take the elevator alone.

When she was eleven, she read *The Diary of Anne Frank* in school, the Scholastic Books version with pages of glossy photographs in the middle. It was then, she thought, looking back, that she had felt her Jewishness, not from the story, though it had moved her, obsessed her, even, in an almost perverse way, so that she half longed to be that girl, to have that garret life, that urgency and bright voice—the way she had wanted, earlier, to be the girl in *The Little Princess,* who was a pauper until her rich father returned. She was not, at the time, really able to consider what happened after the book ended, except as a fairy tale gone wrong, Gretel in the oven with no way out.

No, she had felt Jewish not because she understood the history, but because she *looked* like Anne, with the same sharp chin, the same dark, wavy hair and half-shy, half-playful grin. She had always known that she did not look like most of the girls in her town, who tended to have long, straight blond or brown hair, upturned noses. But when she saw the photo, she thought, *They* would have seen me and known, and then, in a way, perhaps, she did feel the history, for she pictured herself backed against a door with her own face announcing her. In class the next day, the teacher, probably trying in her misguided way to be sensitive, asked Sarah how she had responded to the book. She felt all eyes upon her, an inky rush of shame. She ducked her head, shrugged her shoulders, and the teacher moved on.

Now she got up, went to the bathroom, peed. Usually she peed with the door open even when Tom was there, but this time she shut it. She saw herself then in the full-length mirror, a staring, dark woman with her jeans around her ankles, her knees sticking out. She loved her things, felt her home to be a safer, better place when it was filled with passed-along objects. Did she know, at the same time, that her things each had a history of pain, of labor, or did he have to point that out to her? She looked around her bathroom. Someone once had bent the metal for her old tin box. Someone had mined the ore. Someone had painted the flowers, made the paint, the brush.

She pictured them all in front of her: the paint maker, the brush maker, the miner, watching her watch herself pee. *It's beautiful,* she told them, but the words hung limp and overused inside her head. Was there room, anywhere, for her pleasure in the box's black painted top and deep red flowers, its carefully crafted hinges? In her mind they would not meet her eyes, all those makers. They just stood there and watched until her pee became a trickle, then stopped.

And the desk, people had made that, too, had suffered over it: metal workers, loggers in forests, makers of nails, of glue. And children had seen the swastika—blond Christian children, some who did not understand it, others who thought it either bad or good; Jewish children, if there had been any around here back then. Maybe a German-Jewish girl shipped over to live with a farm family during the war. Perhaps she had lived in the very house where Sarah found the desk, crossed seas and kept her life, only to find, in this Vermont town, a jabbing, spiked cruelty.

It was hard to imagine it all; she knew she could not, really, and yet at the same time, she knew, as she stood up and flushed, that the desk would have to leave. She could not say exactly why, except that the carving glowed neon and fierce now in her mind and the lines she had added seemed a travesty. And even if she could erase the sign, there was her talk with Tom and the way the desk would hold their words like a sponge. Her grandmother had sent her a mezuzah when she graduated from college, to put up over her new door. She knew just where it was, in a small wax envelope in her filing cabinet. She had not put it up because she did not believe in God, not anyone's God. But now she wanted it, as a superstition, a charm, one sign's power over another.

She rinsed her hands and went into the main room. Tom was lying on his back, his eyes shut.

"Okay," she said. "Okay, fine. I want to get rid of it. Help me carry it out."

She didn't need his help, but she wanted it. She put the cactus on the trunk, the flying shuttle and box on the bookcase. He sat up, rubbed his eyes.

"Oh, come on, Sarah. It was just a discussion."

"Help me carry it."

"It's a nice desk. I was playing devil's advocate. You're really going to throw it out? That's ridiculous."

"Just help me carry it out."

He got up and put on his sneakers. They carried it down the stairs; he went backwards and she forwards. The desk was light, and at one point he said he'd just take it on his own, but she didn't answer, and they kept at it the way they had begun, awkward, bumping, lifting it higher to get around corners. Finally they set it down on the front sidewalk.

He lit a cigarette. "I really think you're overreacting. What do we do with it now?"

"Someone will take it," she said, but then she realized she didn't want it on her street, not in her neighborhood, even. She ran upstairs, put on her shoes, and got her keys, then came back down and opened the hatchback of her car.

"Oh God," he said. "Where are you planning to go?"

But she could only shrug.

They put the desk in the car, and then she got in the driver's seat, and he tapped on the other side and she let him in. She didn't know where she was driving, only that she did not want the desk nearby, so she drove to where the houses were single-family, not carved into apartments, and soon she was in the neighborhood where she had found the desk in the first place, and then she made a few deliberate turns and pulled up to the curb by the house with the mansard roof.

"Here?" he said, and she nodded. "How come?"

"I don't know."

He put his hand on the door to get out.

"I've got it, " she said.

She turned off the car and stepped outside. The garbage collectors must have come and gone since she had been there a few hours before; the sidewalk was bare except for a few scraps of paper they had missed, and a squashed piece of wilted lettuce. She took the desk and set it down, its empty mouth facing the house. Maybe the old woman inside the house, or whoever lived there, would come out and see it, oiled but with its legs still rusty, a neat black grid etched on its left-hand corner. She didn't know if she hoped for this, didn't know, either, if she was angry at Tom for lecturing her this way and ruining the desk, or grateful because he had pushed her to get rid of what she now felt to be a cursed object.

She knew, standing there, that things probably wouldn't work out with him. It might take a while to fall apart; he could be so tender, and she felt such a longing for his touch. But she wanted a man who loved wood; it was almost that simple. She wanted a man who walked through the world and saw grain and nap, dirt and oil, a man who cut open green peppers and touched the clusters of fan-shaped seeds, the fuzzed white-stemmed center, the green pockets covered with down like the hair on arms. She wanted someone who followed handmade arrows down dirt roads to places he had never been—a wanderer, a gatherer. It wouldn't work out not because of the sort of talk they had just had, but because of what followed, the fact that he called it a "discussion"—and that now, as she left the desk on the sidewalk, he was saying out the window how crazy this was, she should just keep it, she should put it back in the car.

Standing there, she, who never stopped gathering, never stopped collecting—she, the magpie with her beak full of metal scraps—thought for a moment about leaving them both there: the desk, the man. But she could not drive away without him. It was not his fault; it was, if anything, her own, for she agreed with him now (or at least she thought she did) that she should not have altered the desk.

Anyway, why throw out everything at once? (It sounded like something her grandmother would say.) For a moment she wanted, even, to retrieve the desk, sand it clean of a history which was and was not her own, or put it back the way it was when she found it, etch that jagged sign on again and see if it brought her closer to what was, in the end, unimaginable to her, though she had the quick, dark eyes, the thick, black hair, and the feeling (where did it come from? She refused to believe it was in her blood) that everything, at any moment, might slip away.

Finally, though, she suspected her own reasons. It was so pretty, that desk, when you looked at it in the light, with its arched, antic legs and big feet, its slanted top—like a colt, almost, mahogany and oiled. Get in the car, she told herself, and her hands in front of her were empty, itching. She shut the hatchback, got in the car, drove away.

Charm

Her name was Margy, hard *g,* like *aargh,* or *argonaut.* Not soft *g* like *margarine,* and if someone called her that, she'd show them her disdain. Sometimes her father did it for a laugh, and she'd have to climb into his lap, press her nose to his, and stare at him until he stopped. She hated underpants, took them off the moment she left home. Stashed them in the bushes on the Common, skipped the last few blocks down Beacon Street, breezes playing freely underneath her pleated skirt. Some days she forgot and climbed the jungle gym, leaped off of it whooping, and suddenly her mother would arrive.

"You'll be the death of me," she'd say, holding out another pair of underpants for Margy to step in—then she'd yank them firmly up again. "Why can't you keep them on?"

"They feel obnoxious," Margy would explain, enduring them a moment till her mother left. Then she took them off again.

After school, her mother practiced organ in the cold stone church, while Margy climbed the slippery backs of pews. At home they would sing songs from musicals or off the radio, her mother leaning back and smiling while her fingers rode the keys of the old upright piano in the living room, *The rain in Spain stays mainly in the plain,* and *Suddenly those little eyes will flash and send you thrashing through the wall.* But on the organ, it was Bach and Buxtehude, Handel and hymns, and her mother crouched over the tiered keyboards, one hand stretched to hold a chord while the other flipped a page, or changed the trumpets into piccolos, bare toes on the pedals as the pipes around them roared, shuddering the walls and floors.

Margy tried piano, but she was small for her age, skinny and pale, hair almost white and curled in tiny knots, glasses on her nose—her fingers didn't span five notes. Her mother took her to the symphony, showed her the violins. Margy was not impressed. Violins droned in a swarm like bees, filling in the background of the melody. They whined like hamsters, put out snoring sounds that made her want to snooze.

Then her mother gave her one her size, with a bow. Three strokes on the strings, close up beneath her chin, and she had noticed certain possibilities. This thing could shriek like an ice pick in your ear, and it was portable. You could sneak around a corner, stampede into a room, drown out the piano if you stood on top of it.

"All right, all right," her mother said and cowered back, as Margy stormed into the kitchen, showing her.

Her mother drove her to lessons and, on Saturdays, to music school. Weekdays she practiced in a classroom at lunchtime, while other kids milled uselessly around, pausing on the blacktop underneath the window where she played. Her mother would show up with violin and food, some peculiar sandwich she had made herself, cream cheese with pimentos, peanut butter and bananas on raisin bread. Her mother grew up in Virginia, in a house where other women cooked, and she claimed she couldn't boil water when she married Margy's dad. But she took to cooking ardently and made up recipes, crab baked with mayonnaise in ceramic seashells, cheese sails on potato boats, apples stuffed with walnuts in marshmallow sauce.

Margy ate the crazy food, learned all the squeaks and wails the violin could make. She let herself be dressed in pinafores, driven off to play in little halls with brocade chairs, mothers in white gloves and hats with veils. Sometimes she played in church, echoes crashing onto stone, and once a year before a panel of old men, who scowled over their glasses if she played a piece in double time, or threw in extra fingering to make it sound more interesting.

"Just play the notes on the page," her mother said grimly, driving her away from one audition, where she had received a "Fair" in Interpretation and a "Poor" in Discipline. "Just the notes on the page. Can't you see them there?"

She bought Margy a metronome, made her use it every time she played. She made her stand still practicing, nose-strings-elbow-knee all in one line, and not burst into rooms, leap out of closets fiddling. The year she turned eleven, her mother sent her to charm school, to set her straight on a few things. In an empty classroom after school, with a dozen other girls, she learned to hold a purse in the crook of her arm, clutch gloves by the fingers (not the palm), cross legs at the ankle (not the knee). She learned to say "I'm sorry" and "Excuse me" and "That wasn't what I meant to say," and "I'm afraid that didn't come out quite right." She learned to gain ten pounds. One week they had to take their measurements to class, and the instructor crouched down gracefully beside each desk, whispering advice. Sixty-eight pounds was not enough, she said. Twenty-six inches wasn't much of a chest. She sent Margy home to drink a glass of half-and-half with ginger ale every afternoon, sitting at the table with her mother watching her. Then she would race upstairs, remove her boring uniform, pick up the violin. Their house was solid brick, attached on both sides, with centuries of dust in cracks along the floors—her father was an architect, restored it himself, and he thought it had once been a barracks in the Revolutionary War. But standing on a chair at the head of the stairs, she could shudder it from attic to basement with shock waves of violin.

"What hath God wrought?" her father said one day, gazing up the stairs at her as he came in, though he had been raised by devout New England atheists and did not go to church at all.

One day after school, her mother was not there. Her father came home early, took her out for hamburgers. Just a little operation, he said, she'd be all right in a few weeks. *Weeks?* Margy thought, and eyed the empty house. She took the violin into the hospital, but the nurses said her mother wasn't ready yet to hear her play. Her mother lay as flat as if her bones were gone, bandages from neck to knee, smelling of alcohol. Her face was white and thin, her eyes slid off of Margy's when they tried to look at her. Margy gripped her shoulder once to stress a point (*Come home at once*), and her mother's mouth opened, pink with a black hole in back, let out a high thin note. A nurse rushed in, took Margy out.

Her grandmother came from Virginia, cooked for them, closed the door to Margy's room when she was practicing. Her mother came home for a week, thin and strangely brown, soft hair vanished underneath a wig of gleaming strands, pale and all one color like the horsehair used in bows. Then she was gone again. One day her grandmother came to school, took Margy out.

She would always have her mother now, her grandmother said. She would always be there, looking out for her. Only somewhat invisible, because God had wanted her too much.

"God," Margy said, for approximately the last time in her life.

At the funeral, the organ was silent, like a riderless horse. Her father towered next to her, no part of him moving, eyes open on the prayers. Her grandmother draped both her heavy arms around Margy's shoulders, exuding softness and lavender, easing her head down toward the floor. Margy studied the flagstones, listened to the shuffling and sniffling, the rumbling in her grandmother's throat, forever and ever, father, son, and ghost.

Her grandmother stayed on a few more weeks, taught her to dust and clean, scrub vegetables, cook bacon, wash her father's clothes. Then she went home, and Margy was on her own. After school, when her father was gone, she'd practice violin, go through his desk, eat sugar cubes. For dinner she cooked things she knew: spaghetti with tomato sauce, grilled-cheese sandwiches, canned peas. Once, she put her hand down on the stove and burned it black, smelled it searing like a steak. White ridges of the fingerprints rose past the char, a blueprint or road map.

"Electric burners can be dangerous," her father said, examining the bandage she had made. He was fond of practical details, built his own models, and sometimes Margy helped, gluing tiny trees of crepe paper to paper grass, around the cardboard buildings he designed. He taught her to clean counters (feeling with the fingers, not the sponge), compare the different brands of food (weight as well as price). When she ironed his pants with creases to the sides, he showed her the right way. It was his looks she'd gotten, almost albino with pale translucent skin, though he was tall, his tight curls faintly red. Now he focused on her hand.

"It's going to hurt for days," he said.

"It's all right," Margy said, took back her hand, though it was throbbing to the elbow at the time. She couldn't play the violin for weeks. But then she could, and she carried it to school in its case, to practice at lunch hour with no one listening.

The spring she was fourteen, the Common filled with hippies, in dirty feet and jewels in their noses and even naked flopping breasts, whirling on the grass and staring at the sun, or even writhing underneath some smelly hippie guy—Margy would avert her eyes, passing in her blue-check uniform. She wore underpants these days, and knew certain things for sure: she had good taste. She was not cheap. Boys would have to crawl through flames to get to her. And if a few girls that she knew seemed destined for life out on the Common (rolling skirts up to the crotch, penciling their eyes with kohl, smoking marijuana in the ladies' room), Margy avoided them. She practiced violin, in perfect time without a metronome, every sinew tuned to play vibrato, tremolo, vicious fingering by Mozart, Paganini, Brahms.

Then one day a girl that she had known since they were five, who sometimes wore her Girl Scout uniform to school, wrote her a note to say that she was having sex. Karen was a round, contented blonde, like several others to whom Margy had attached herself—"Margy's Brunhildes," her mother had called them, because none of them had learned to walk till they were three, and they spent their afternoons in ruffled bedrooms, eating cupcakes, making up for Margy's meager twitchiness with gorgeous amplitude. Margy and Karen wrote notes in Math when they were bored, usually about the unclean uniform on the girl in front of them, or people that they knew from music school, where Karen played a desultory flute. Today Margy had to read the note three times, the room around her spangled in strange light. At the board, the math teacher droned on about Pythagoras and pi.

"What was it like?" she scrawled, fingers trembling. "Painful?" she added, folded the note up, and waited for Mr. Bobbio to turn around. From the side of her eye, she could see Karen at the desk across the aisle, watching the board with round blue eyes, pageboy smooth against her cheek like a little Dutch girl in a tulip field.

"Only at first," the note came back. "Then it was nice. You won't believe how good it felt by the second or third time."

Margy slid down in her seat, trying not to breathe unusually. Her mother had of course described the procreative act to her, but so gruesomely she had assumed that it must happen in a doctor's office, under medical supervision, only a few times in your life—though even then the logic of the thing had worried her. She knew her mother had had five miscarriages before she was born, and that her parents had decided to stop trying to have kids, when Margy "came along."

"The birth control we had in those days wasn't very good," her mother had explained, avoiding her eyes. "So you happened in spite of it."

"Why didn't you just *not do it*?" Margy had suggested firmly, having put up with all the foolishness she could.

Her mother seemed to freeze on this question.

"It's an expression of love," she said, but so stiffly Margy knew something was wrong with this. She hadn't given it much thought in the intervening time. But now here was Karen's note, saying, "It makes me go all gooey like a toasted marshmallow, just to remember it."

Mr. Bobbio was drifting near her desk, his hair half gray, half black, standing up on one side, black eyes shining ecstatically. Sometimes he forgot about Pythagoras and told them about World War II, in which he had flown planes. Margy stared up at him, willing him to take a trip to the Calvados zone.

"You always know where you are with geometry," he said, gazing down at her. Lightly he rapped his knuckles on her desk, inches from the note. "No flailing in the dark. The numbers are either there, or they're not."

Margy's lips parted, she gave him a small understanding smile—for a moment he stared back as if entranced. Face clearing, he whirled back to the board.

"How big does it get?" she wrote. "How often does it happen? How long does it take?"

They never wrote about it anywhere but Math. Other teachers were too alert, known to read the notes that fell into their hands, and though they gave each other significant looks at lunch and in Phys. Ed., they never mentioned it out loud. But that spring Margy learned a great deal in Geometry. Familiar words revealed themselves in a new and startling light: to come, to pull out, to go down. When the man comes, when the woman comes. When come has a "the" in front of it. She also learned new words she'd never heard, short and punchy, or with luscious rolling sounds. She was not used to learning things from Karen. Margy got better grades, and Karen sometimes had to copy from her tests. Margy won all of their fights. A few years before, they'd had a screaming argument, about the number of secret openings in the female body. They had just seen the film about those special times they could look forward to having soon, and Karen thought the movie had implied a third, between the two they knew. Out on the asphalt after school, she drew a diagram in hopscotch chalk, three holes in a vertical line. Margy drew a rival next to it, with only two, and applied some crushing logic: How could there be room? Why did you need it, for such a minor event? Faces hot, both shrieked at once—till Karen began to falter. Blinking, bewildered, she'd accepted defeat.

"It better not come out as fast as I usually pee," she said, looking worried for the first time.

Now Margy asked the questions, Karen answered them. (*Big as a cardboard toilet paper roll. Half an hour, maybe less. Any time we like.*) At the end of every class, Karen grandly handed her the notes, and Margy locked them up inside the blue velvet pocket of her violin case, to study later on. The trees on Beacon Street lushed out in pale green leaf, the air warm and sweet with whiffs of river rot just lately thawed from ice, as they joined the flood of girls after school in blue plaid uniforms. Karen rode with her car pool, back to her ruffled room, where her boyfriend would converge from the boys' school across town, bringing foam or rubbers or his mother's diaphragm, whatever he had managed to secure. Karen's mother ate late lunches out and liked to shop, have her hair combed out, and drink tea with friends. Karen's father did not live with them, and Mrs. Snyder went out frequently at night, sometimes in strapless gowns, smelling of hand-mixed powder by Charles of the Ritz and perfume. Once she had come into Margy's house to use the phone, and for three days afterwards it smelled like Joy de Jean Patou. Karen was always in her bed alone, asleep, when her mother came back home.

Margy practiced violin, made dinner for her father and herself. Three nights a week she had rehearsal with Youth Orchestra, next door to the Boston Symphony, and Karen showed up, too, a little late most nights, with fresh red cheeks, body languid as a smile, lips too bruised to form an embouchure.

Youth Orchestra was a chaotic scene, prima donnas from the little halls of brocade chairs, boys from Catholic School who smoked out on the fire escape and made rude noises on their instruments. The soloist on this year's Mozart was the older brother of a kid they knew from music school. Jason Slade was shorter than Margy, shaped like a brick, and snide—Margy had known him since they were six, and never seen him smile. But his older brother, Gary, was tall and handsome, graceful as a tulip from the bulb of Jason Slade, and he knew how to smile. He went to Latin School, played piano instead of violin, and in the fall he would be going to Juilliard. These days at music school, Margy played piano for her second instrument, but she knew she sounded literal and childish next to him. As the concert date got close, she watched him almost every night, long hands floating across the keys, long back dipping gently to the beat, as if nodding in the breeze.

One night on rehearsal break, three trumpeters stood in her way as she approached the Coke machine. Irish boys from Catholic School, their leader long and lean in painfully tight jeans, red hair slicked high into a point over his forehead like a cresting wave, though most young men these days wore theirs like Bobby Kennedy, or Gary Slade, clean and loose, washed every day. Jackson was the redhead's name, and he leered down at Margy with his thin pink face, so close that she could catch the fake-mint odor on his hair.

"The Princess Margaret," he said, while his henchmen lounged beside him, watching her. "Ice queen of the strings."

Margy pulled her nose back from the smell. "What is that on your hair, Brylcreem?"

The three boys chuckled to themselves. Jackson spread his hands.

"Ladies and gentlemen, I owe it all to Brylcreem. Gives me just the right amount of slip in those tight moments."

The henchmen snickered, quivering excitedly, and Jackson wedged a finger in the pocket of his jeans to wheedle out a long wide comb. Fascinated, Margy watched.

"You had a *comb* in there?" she said, as Jackson extracted it, smoothed back his insulted hair. One of the henchmen leaned toward her. He was short and dark, trying to grow a mustache, lonely black hairs here and there on his upper lip.

"Yeah, and he's got something else in there for you besides."

Margy recoiled, turned back the way she came, and bounced into the soft Shetland sweater on the chest of Gary Slade.

"Shut up, McCarthy," said a deep voice above her head. Long hands enclosed her shoulders, turned her away. Gary Slade led her to a spot on the black metal stairs, above the crowd in the hallway. He brought her a Coke, apologized for Jackson and McCarthy.

"Brass players. An unfortunate necessity, but hormonal cretins all the same. Try to ignore them."

He sat lightly next to her until the end of break, hands resting between his knees, asking polite questions about her school, her music teacher, who she knew, and on the next few nights, he brought her other Cokes, waited out front until her father came to pick her up. One night her father was late, and Gary took her hand, touched the calluses along the fingerpads.

"I see you've been practicing like a good girl," he said and laughed, lightly kissed them one by one.

Margy was too happy to speak, too happy to discuss it with anyone. She especially didn't mention it to Karen, who might have turned it into toilet paper rolls, and how to tell when it was time to make the man pull out. She was happy in the morning, opening her eyes, the yellow light in her bedroom, the promise of rehearsal later on. Even the dust motes in the air were beautiful, the smell of mothballs from the house on the corner where the two old ladies lived. The hippies frolicking across the Common seemed innocuous and innocent, and when they asked her for change, she gave them what she had.

"Isosceles," she said and beamed at Mr. Bobbio, the day she noticed the beauty of the triangle. So simple, so clear—no flailing in the dark! The numbers always came out evenly!

"Yes!" he cried, his half-gray mane electrified. "Yes, you see! You get it now!"

The night before the final test in Math, Margy stayed up half the night to learn a month's worth from the book, and by the next afternoon, she had forgotten most of it, though Karen faithfully copied what she wrote. That week her father had to take a trip, and he arranged for her to stay at Karen's house. It was the last week of rehearsal with Youth Orchestra, the concert coming up on Friday night, and he promised to be back in time for it.

On Monday Margy packed a bag, went home with Karen after school. Karen's house was in Jamaica Plain, a wide brick split-level with big French doors that radiated cold for six months of the year, and every room was done in powder blue, with plush rugs, quilted wallpaper, satin-striped loveseats. Karen's boyfriend did not appear that afternoon, with Margy there, and Karen seemed bored, showing off her stash of birth control, soaking in bubble bath until rehearsal time.

She had told her mother they'd be riding to rehearsal with the parents of another girl, but since Mrs. Snyder was not home, her boyfriend picked them up a whole hour before rehearsal time. They dropped Margy at the empty hall, and by the time Karen got back the orchestra had filled the chairs, milled through warmup, settled down, and was torturing the opening of the Beethoven. The conductor glared across the stage, but Karen did not glance his way, sliding into place with the flutes.

Gary asked if he could drive Margy back to Karen's house that night. When Margy told her, Karen widened her round eyes, looked slightly scandalized, and disappeared.

"Karen Snyder is a nice girl," Gary said, as they drove away in his parents' car. "But possibly a little bit naive. And not as talented as you."

He drove out past Jamaica Plain along a wooded road, and parked the car in the dark. Up close he smelled like English Leather, clean skin and ironed shirt. Margy was aware of his heartbeat, the prickle at the edge of his smooth lips, the warmth inside his mouth—while at the same time she was leaping off of cliffs, discovering that she could fly. She was playing on a stage in Yankee Stadium, fifty thousand people throwing roses and star lilies, Leonard Bernstein on his knees.

Gradually a chill crept in the car. When she opened her eyes, the darkness seemed less dense, more clear, though Gary had removed her glasses long before. She sat up straighter, breaking his hold.

"I should get back. Mrs. Snyder will think I've been kidnapped."

He kept his arms around her, face down in her neck. "Maybe you have been. Girl violinist kidnapped in Jamaica Plain. Symphony joins girl hunt, beating with bows."

Margy chuckled, rested her forehead a moment on his shirt. It was time to go—she pulled a little farther back.

In the dim light from the road, Gary watched her, arching one sandy brow. His free hand reached toward the steering wheel. Slipping the car keys from the ignition, he tucked them in one graceful movement down inside his fine-wale tan cords.

"Whoops. Did you see that?"

Margy chuckled, watching him. He looked at her pleasantly.

"Well, we have a problem here. We can't go anyplace till somebody gets the keys. You saw where they went, didn't you? I'm afraid you'll have to put your hand in there and get them out."

"Oh, sure," Margy said and laughed.

"You may laugh, you may joke, ha ha," Gary said. "But the fact remains, we won't leave here until you get the keys."

Obscurely she imagined the inside of his pants—nothing Karen said helped now, and she could only picture it as something like her own, cold skin that never saw the light, little secret hairs, parts that needed scrupulous washing. His parents' car was big and wide, and the seat back popped with static sparks as she slid closer to the door.

"Gary. We have to go."

"Sure," he said, sliding after her. "We'll go. But first you have a job to do. Here, I'll make it easy for you."

Reaching down with both hands, he undid the top button of his pants. Breathing on her neck, he shifted on the seat, lifting his crotch to graze her arm.

The door handle felt cold and loose as Margy fumbled for it in the dark—jerking it, she burst out of the car. The sudden motion of the night was a surprise, a breeze swinging wires, black leaves nodding against splashes of light. Loafers slapping on asphalt, she ran down a hill, out of sight of the fat car. She'd left her glasses on the dash, and objects farther than a few feet off were blurred into one plane. But across the road, she could remember woods, with

Boston on the other side. Dashing across, she climbed the bank, slipping to her knees in the wet grass.

Streetlight faintly lit the trees, as branches zigzagged toward her face, senseless as a drawing by Picasso or Braque. Then it was dark in a way the Back Bay never was, and she had to hold her hands before her eyes to ward off twigs. She knew about woods mainly by rumor. Her mother had never let her go to camp, but once she was a tree in *The Nutcracker,* holding a spangled branch above her head while she did *petits pas* across the stage. That time she had not been alone, and where to go was chalked along the floor. The music told her when to move. This time there was no sound but her own breath, and the secret shush of leaves.

The wide brick houses had a military look, like bunkers guarding missiles in the dark, and none of them were lit. Her loafers were fine as glove leather, had cost her half a year's allowance, but they hung heavy now with mud. Shuffling up and down the blocks, she peered without her glasses in the dark, until she found the house she thought was right, though the front door was locked. The back gate groaned, and she clattered into a chaise longue. Holding her breath, she crept up to the French doors in back, and lights burst on inside.

Mrs. Snyder stood behind the glass, eyes unnaturally wide. She had on a pink peignoir and nightgown, her hair puffed in a satin cap, and she was hiding something behind her back. Perfume rolled out the doors as she opened them, made little jerking motions with her head, told Margy to get in. Did she realize that it was four a.m.? Did she realize this was a gun in her hand?

"I don't want to scare you," she said. "But this is a gun in my hand."

Mrs. Snyder let her sleep a few hours on a loveseat, so as not to wake Karen. Then she took her home before Karen could wake up. Driving in the station wagon through the bright May dawn, she said it was too bad, but she felt sure that Margy understood. Mrs. Snyder was already groomed, in a pink sweater set, pearls, and powder, shellpink lipstick applied with a brush. In the morning light, her hair was fair as Karen's, all one shade, like the wig that Margy's mother had once used. Margy sat still in her ruined shoes.

"Maybe it's because you lost your mother," Mrs. Snyder said. "Girls have gone wild before because of that. I feel for you, I really do. But I have my own girl to protect. You understand."

She could not let Karen go on being friends with her. Karen's grades were suffering, and the math teacher had even called to say she'd cheated on a test, and Margy was involved.

"Now this. It's just too much." She had called Margy's father at his hotel in New York. He was cutting short the trip, would be home by dinnertime. She drove into the streets of the Back Bay, stopped in front of Margy's house. Tipping her head to one side, she gave Margy a small smile.

"You could set that hair of yours, you know. Tame that curl down. You're not a bad-looking girl. You could be all right."

Margy wore her old bent glasses to the last rehearsals, and a turtleneck, though it failed to cover up the purple bruises on her neck. On the left, where the violin pressed to her skin, they might have passed for signs of vigorous practicing. But they were on the right, bloomed in plain sight like horrible mushrooms, blue with red veins and painful to the touch, though she hadn't felt him giving them to her. Every eye that passed over her face slid down an inch and paused. The conductor's eyes surveyed the violins, and lingered on her neck. The boy on her right, who smelled like old cheese, shot so many sweaty looks her way that he lost his place, came in two measures early on the Beethoven.

Gary strolled to the piano for his solo and returned to his place in back without a glance her way. Karen did not stop to say hello, or sit with her in Math. She wore her Girl Scout uniform to school, and was on time for orchestra. Rehearsal breaks were shorter now, quick trips to the bathroom or the Coke machine, and Karen stayed in her seat, turned her pageboy under with her hands as she talked to the girl next to her. Once, Margy came back to the room and saw Gary crouched by Karen's side. A moment later, Karen threaded through the chairs, slipped the missing glasses into Margy's lap, and turned away.

"Here," she whispered, not even looking at her face, as if the glasses were a knife with blood on it, or soiled underpants.

Concert night, Gary and Jason Slade were giving a party after the show. They lived in Brookline, had a pool, and everyone seemed to be going except Margy. In the locker room, a cellist Margy knew showed her the red bikini underneath her concert clothes.

"This damn thing," she said, wriggling to pull it down in back. "Makes lousy underwear. But nothing's going to stop me getting in that pool."

Margy had drawn an inside chair, next to the abyss of the audience, and in her required white-blouse-black-skirt, the marks on her neck must have been discernible up to the second balcony. Past the lights, she heard the breathing of five hundred parents, grandparents, uncles, cousins, aunts, every time she lifted up her bow. But ten minutes after their cheerful dumb encore (the same scherzo they had done the year before), the building drained of life, except for Margy and the cheese-smelling boy, plus twenty or so desperate nerds who cried if you looked at them, standing in the lobby with their parents drinking punch. Margy was stunned with misery. Her father had been kind to her all week, not mentioning her neck, or Mrs. Snyder, or four a.m., and tonight he had dressed up in a Windsor jacket worthy of Sherlock Holmes, belted in orangish-brown plaid that clashed with his hair, matching pants, and freshly polished brown wingtips. Raising his eyebrows, he offered various remarks.

"Great concert. Glad it's over with? Any of these kids your friends?"

"Not really," Margy managed to say. "Can we please go?"

Her father seemed deflated. "Then who are your friends?"

She went backstage to get her clothes. In the echoing wings, a girl laughed somewhere, and a door slammed. Then it was so quiet she could hear the metal of the stair rail tick as she climbed to the locker rooms. She was almost to the top when Jackson and McCarthy burst out through the swinging doors, laughing so their eyes were slits.

"Well, I do declare," Jackson said. Smelling flammable, they stood at the head of the stairs.

"Well, well," said McCarthy, and tried to hang a cigarette from his lower lip—falling, it glanced off his chest and down the stairs. With a flourish, Jackson slid one out of his own pack, lit it, placed it tenderly in his friend's lips. Margy tried to slip past them.

"Not so fast," Jackson said, one arm shooting out to block her path. From his pocket, he extracted a glass flask. "Here's to your neck."

"Your neck!" McCarthy cried, exhaling an enthusiastic cloud.

Jackson wiped the top of the flask with his sleeve, and held it out. "You are a much nicer girl than we thought. Such a goddamn lot of virgins in this orchestra."

McCarthy nodded vigorously. "Like that ice bitch, Karen Snyder, your frigid friend. Hers is made of leather, I understand. Thanks be to the Heavenly Father, Margy Rose, and let us sing to you, for not being one of them."

Margy felt a sudden rushing in her veins, like a train toward a brick wall. She took the flask from Jackson's hand. The first sip hurt, then it felt good.

"Okay," she said, a twisted croak. She cleared her throat. "Okay, let's hear you sing. Can you sing, McCarthy, for your poontang? How do you boys like it, anyway? Face to face, or maybe in the rear, the Catholic way? Let's get those jeans off now, and see what you can do. Let's see those dangerous dicks. Big and hard, are they, or suitable to satisfy a toy poodle?"

McCarthy and Jackson seemed to have lost the ability to move. In the fluorescent light of the stairwell, every hair and pimple glared against the pallor of their skin.

"You know," she said. "Cunt teasing is just as bad as the other kind. Worse, actually, when you haven't got the balls to turn blue. Have you boys worn out your weenies jerking off today, or are you ready to screw?"

"You'd better watch..." Jackson began faintly, his voice trailing off. Taking the bottle from her hand, he glanced around to see if anyone was listening, stepped down a few stairs. McCarthy followed him.

"What I really want to know is, do you boys have foreskins? In my survey of American males, it seems to me that circumcision has become awfully popular lately, and I'd like to see one of those floppy little hoods if I ever get the chance. Do they do it to little Catholics? Put the knife right on that tender tip and slice it off of you?"

Jackson and McCarthy turned, shoulders lightly touching. At the bottom of the stairs, they pushed out through the exit door, a gust of giggles blowing back as it swung closed. Margy rushed behind them, as far as the fire escape, trying to make use of her full vocabulary. She hit on some happy phrases by the end, but Jackson and McCarthy were gone, and her last remarks were wasted on brick walls, plus a pair of parents walking up the alleyway, a boy with a French horn between them as if on a leash. The woman's hair was short and brisk, and she passed so close Margy could smell her perfume, something sugary and green, not Joy de Jean Patou.

The woman stared up at her, eyes glowing in the dark: You'll be the death of someone, they said. Does your mother know where you are?

I don't *have* a mother, Margy thought, with a sudden leap of heart. No mother she could hurt with what she did, or appall, or please. Somehow for two years she'd gone on expecting her, as if she were about to show up with a pair of underpants. But her mother wasn't on her way, and Margy could go naked underneath her clothes, play double time or with the metronome. Become a Girl Scout in a diaphragm, or only sound like one. Or she could try to play at Yankee Stadium.

The little family retreated to the street, turned the corner out of sight. Margy tried the door of the fire escape. But it was locked from the inside, and she had to walk around the building in the warm night air, proceed by the front doors into the bright lights of the lobby, where her father was waiting.

Alice, Australia

In the cinder-block waiting room
There was nothing but canteen machines
And a rack of benches.
Outside it began to rain.
Another passenger came in.
He said the girls in the opposite bar
Were getting drunk and dirty.
Suddenly one stumbled in with her drunken john,
Her hair and dress drenched. She tilted
Her neck to let the rain drip off, wearing
A gauze kite of a dress and felt go-go boots.
You could see her white underwear—
Bandages, pieces of adhesive tape. The pair
Ignored us, turned their backs toward us,
And standing over by the canteen machines
She pulled out his thing and started to jerk it
With a rhythm I had never seen between humans,
As if pumping water from a well
Or teaching a dog how to heel or sit
By tugging its leash, snapping her wrist
As if she believed any one shot would ring the bell.
It was ugly, disgusting, and probably painful,
Her john humped over as if half-unconscious
But trying to pull away or steel himself
For an inner convulsion. I tried to listen
To the drill of rain and mind my own business,
Or say something witty about the gap
Between tempo and tune, but the spectacle
Tied my tongue in a knot. I went out
To look down the track for signs of my train.
It was pouring like absolute hell,
But I saw the engine's yellow eye,

Heard it pant, and then with its gnashing
Of brakes, scream of steam and wheels of steel
On steel, it was there. All aboard I was glad
For my quiet compartment and relative sanity,
Thinking of Emily Dickinson's white dress,
Or Miss Habersham in Dickens's *Great Expectations*
To elevate my revery, when I was joined
By a gray-haired man with a familiar air.
"You're the girl," I murmured. "I saw you
Wearing a wedding dress short as a nightie." He shrugged
And informed me calmly, "Nothing to fear.
That's how things are in Alice, Australia,
Out on the new frontier!"

Invisible City

Hasn't everyone lived in an invisible
And essentially unreal, imaginary city
With beautiful empty buildings on byways
Or sewers called canals filled with
Slopping water and huge coffins offering
Pronged upright musical clefs to the air
As the whole load staggers nobly
Toward the extraordinary, and maybe Venice
Was named for Venus, the gondola
For someone gone over the edge,
Poled politely up and down with art
By fellows in straw hats and jerseys,
Warehouses, churches, and meeting places,
A Bridge of Sighs where lovers and prisoners
Are still confused and identical as in
D. H. Lawrence's mating of whales poem where
Archangels of bliss cross over a bull's
Let's call it his Bridge of Sighs,
For in clandestine Venice, as if named
For Venus, although no whales, there are
Waves of blindness, or a gaudy bondage
To which one submits, and life draws
All its lumens from that bridge.

Living with Monkeys

It's not a nice thing.
Not a nice idea. Or it might be
a nice idea. Who knows? King Kong.
Mighty Joe Young. Cheetah.
But it's not nice, not really.
Living with monkeys is not pretty.
Beside the quart of chocolate milk
(which had to be divided equally,
my brothers and sister slowly measuring),
live worms in plastic containers
were kept bean-dip–style in the refrigerator
because a monkey likes to eat such things,
and it pleased my father to please a monkey.
They were all his idea, after the guinea pigs
had eaten their offspring, and we had
lost the parrot, abandoned the alligator.
Sometimes they can die pretty quickly.
One did of TB, all animal ethereal,
looking like Mother Theresa, like Gandhi,
swaddled in white towels, and rocked
to its end by my mother who hated it
and who couldn't stop from weeping
over this, her last and strangest baby.
The other thrived on special treats.
Sometimes my brothers gave it something
dazzling to eat (a locust or a lizard)
and would watch happily
as the littlest hands in the family
ripped up little living things.
Oh, they had little hands, little nails,
eyelids, eyelashes, and their eyes
beyond reason, human, inhuman.

Do you know what it's like
to look a monkey eye to eye?
A real monkey who likes to bite,
who will challenge you to fight
for your food or your right to pass by?
Why would anyone think this was good?
How long could this life be withstood?
When my father parted ways with the family,
we knew what to do: leave that monkey outside!
In his cage, he stayed, cold and unclean,
as we went on our desperate first dates,
coming home to smoke dope as we sat in the swings
of the rusty swing set left by a younger family
in the rented backyard full of yellow thistles
and anonymous, vicious little dogs
who liked to fly up and bite
down our clothes from the clothesline.
And when the last monkey finally died,
and the dogs had run away,
and our cat had run away,
we knew what to do: we changed
jobs, changed schools, left friends,
and moved closer to the ocean,
so we could start all over again.

NIN ANDREWS

What Is It About the Past

the Old Country where the children we were
walk around in black and white
movies, long nights with bugs
flying in my window, dreams
slippery as wet fish, moans
in the air from our parents' room? Horses

kicked at their stalls, heat
shivered in the summer skies. Sleepless
we held our breath, saw shadows
come to life and pulled them inside
us, shutting our eyes. I denied
they existed, denied

we existed, remembering the nuns
at school who wore black to hide
their whiteness, wore black
to show us they were servants
of God. I still dream them at night
lifting their heavy gowns
as the past unreels, a soundless
movie on a white wall with nobody watching.

NIN ANDREWS

Secondhand Smoke

After he left, even the topography
shifted. Overnight our seaside resort
became winter dusk in Detroit. Tall buildings
stared me down, and like rush hour denizens
pressed their gray bodies against mine. Their shadows
quivered in my windows and coffee cups
and tasted of secondhand smoke. Like me,
they were all insomniacs. One corporate center
confessed it had always wanted to open
its windows, empty its offices and corridors
of paper and plastic furniture, just lift off,
the wind blowing through its hollow stairwells.
Were it to open one window at a time, you would hear
its soul like a flute or maybe
a clarinet. The funeral parlor on Sixth Street
was afraid of heights. It had dreams
of sailing away with the cathedral at Chartres.
Always in love with Gothic sorts, especially those bedecked
with gargoyles, I imagined sinking slowly, watching
the fish enter the chapel, feeling the pulse
of warm waves and sand at my feet. There are spaces
in things and spaces between that hold the color
of sorrow, the soundless movie no one watches, playing
and playing on our walls. They understood
better than anyone the strain of memories,
his footsteps on their perfect tile. And how
I could not follow, and they held me there
in their yellow light.

The Right Kind

There was this cock in high school,
not that I had anything to do with it
but we girls talked a lot, giggled,
how it had a job to do and was often seen
rising behind its spandex suit
at the country club. It worked pretty good,
we figured, but there was this one girl
who took up complaining about it, like it was a meal
that was too well-done, the service sloppy.
Too quick and not enough of it, that was her
joke, especially when we drove through McD's
on Friday nights. She'd punch out her pill
and take it with a swig of Coke, then talk
about who was in charge of it, how it
could be handled, and later, when her back
was turned, we all whispered
about her, how she wasn't
the right kind of girl, and it wasn't
the right kind of cock.

DANIEL BOURNE

After the Cold War

Sacred day of rain, the crowds on Karol's Bridge
thin out, slightly repentant
of their tourist ways, hunker down
in pensions and hotels,
to ponder the weird twists of language
to be found in their brochures, or complain
of the thinness of the towels,

or of the pickpockets who speak
the quick language of the fingers. Meanwhile,
slowly, very slowly, each sad and slow vowel of stone
in the black figures lining the sides of Karol's Bridge
starts up a keening wail, so long it is longer
than all the twisting streets in Prague,
so difficult to translate
even the smartest translators would despair.

"Beware, beware," each statue mouth says
to the other statue's ear. "This may be our last century
to stand on this bridge. This may be when it happens
in a twinkling of an eye. A sacred day of rain,
the human flesh thinned out, repentant, groping
through the dark halls of their hotels,
and the great mushroom rotting within us,
will finally break open." But,

to the faulty ears of humans, it just
sounds like a wail, an air raid siren
in a world supposedly at peace. Heads
of families from Vermont, from Hamburg,
from a small village near Stockholm,

run out into the street. "What is that noise?"
they are asking. And no one dreams

of the statues on the bridge. Their mouths
open and howling, their hearts
crumbling like limestone
exposed. And inside them, a fungus,
the exhaustion of stone, the secret war more virulent
than K Mart or Marx.

Flood Warning for Warsaw, Late Eighties,
No Political Metaphors

Recent downpour, the black streets glisten,
the red and white bus dips down like a sail
into the runoff pooled near the tram tracks.

Fifteen stories above, I drink beer, floating
in my own sea—the smell of mushrooms
frying in the kitchen—while the dark spike

of the Palace of Culture
fades into the blackness of
yet another Polish night. Yes,

it has rained here for hours, inside and out.
The streets so long to travel, and the steps
I would have to take

to reach you
as you stand by the window
are longer than I can make. On the other side

of the ocean, years later, we may remember
the smell of frying food, the setting in of hard rain,
the flood of the Vistula River. We may remember

but this doesn't help us now, our fatal
attempt to cross
from one side to the other.

THOMAS CENTOLELLA

The Raptors

I've seen them all over the city. After midnight
near the consulate, closer to the streetlight
than you might expect: a parked car, windows misted,
wings for a trademark. And the muffled urgencies
from the back seat—someone about to die, perhaps,
or be delivered—the sleek silhouette of a woman's legs
lifted and spread behind the fogged glass,
and between her legs, a slow moving, a denser kind
of fog... Or outside the bus terminal late in the day,
at commuter peak, the sedan that sat illicitly
by the crosswalk, the jowly man in the driver's seat
going nowhere for now: head back, eyes closed, mouth
open like a slaughtered pig's, while his companion worked
her blond head over his lap, and a thousand people off work
too intent on getting home even to notice.

But we never took that route, that strange craving
to be caught in the act, have others confirm our willingness
to trust reasons that reason itself could never explain.
When she came to me it was for moments
she couldn't claim well enough on her own to keep,
and I took her to where the world endured, the elements
held sway. The small town a temblor had ruined,
blocks of exposed foundations that went deep.
A houseboat where, twice a day, high tide kept us buoyant.
And the coastal road with its blind turns that ended in air
and dared us to keep going, to live that vista.
Whatever we were looking for seemed to find us,
and the only ones to bear witness were a solitary
egret, a yellow moon, the stripped-naked limbs of eucalyptus.

And once, off a high trail, after a warm rain,
her face gleaming, eyes intent, nipples showing
through her soaked blouse, she pressed me against a tree,
said, "I like holding it in my hand," before she took me
into her mouth, one rapt creature at fullest power, feeding
on another. And the pale mountain flowers, barely-there
pinks and blues, like colors for the unborn children
we'd only dream about—these are what she drew
all over her letters later, like another language
altogether, as if words alone couldn't be trusted,
couldn't do justice to that kind of need.
While above us that day, as above us now, lazing
on their massive, recurring thermals: the raptors,
seemingly at play, but raking the valley floor
for anything alive and there for the taking,
anything worth killing for.

The Orders

One spring night, at the end of my street
God was lying in wait.

A friend and I were sitting in his new sedan
like a couple of cops on surveillance,
shooting the breeze to pass the time,
chatting up the daydreams, the raw deals,
all the woulda-coulda-shoulda's,
the latest "Can you believe that?"
As well as the little strokes of luck,
the so-called triumphs, small and unforeseen,
that kept us from cashing it all in.

And God, who's famous for working
in mysterious ways and capable of anything,
took the form of a woman and a man,
each dressed in dark clothes and desperate enough
to walk up to the car and open the doors.

And God put a gun to the head of my friend—
right against the brain stem, where the orders go out
not only to the heart and the lungs
but to consciousness itself—a cold muzzle aimed
at where the oldest urges still have their day:
the one that says eat whatever's at hand,
the one that wants only to fuck,
the one that will kill if it has to . . .

And God said not to look at him
or he'd blow us straight to kingdom come,
and God told us to keep our hands
to ourselves, as if she weren't that kind of girl.

Suddenly time was nothing,
our lives were cheap, the light in the car
cold, light from a hospital,
light from a morgue. And the moments
that followed—if that's what they were—
arrived with a nearly unbearable weight,
until we had acquired
a center of gravity
as great as the planet itself.

My friend could hardly speak—
he was too busy trying not to die—
which made me chatter all the more,
as if words, even the most ordinary ones,
had the power to return us to our lives.

And behind my ad-libbed incantation,
my counterspell to fear, the orders
still went out: keep beating, keep breathing,
you are not permitted to disappear,

even as one half of God kept bitching
to the other half that we didn't have
hardly no money at all, and the other half barked,
"I'm telling you to shut your mouth!"
and went on rummaging through the back seat.
And no one at all looking out their window,
no one coming home or going out . . .

Until two tall neighbors came walking toward us
like unsuspecting saviors . . . And God grabbed
the little we'd been given, the little we still had,
and hustled on to the next dark street.

Little Girl in Blue, 1918

The girl in a blue dress is standing
on pink tile and gazing back at the artist
as if looking through him for a place
to rest. The day is brilliant
with Mediterranean light Modigliani fled
for the gravity of dark hotels,
human throats elongated like sunflowers
on the back streets of Paris, barefoot
girls—this girl who glances suggestively
from the corner as if a dot in the distance
of another life—who seems about to smile;
and the artist who tugs his brush, wonders
if he can endure TB without cocaine
or brandy, coughing only to palm
the rusty blossom of his chest. The girl
fidgets under plumes of smoke
amid the ashes and empty bottles.
She thinks of trees, how green branches
hang in mournful streamers
as little cubes and pyramids of light
tumble over leaves. The story
of this path to the studio, the artist who
she understands is dying, how
he's sketched blue walls around her,
how one blank eye looks inward
and the other out toward mercy.

Clever and Poor

She has always been clever and poor,
    Especially here off the Yugoslav

Train on a platform of dust. Clever was
    Her breakfast of nutmeg ground in water

In place of rationed tea. Poor was the cracked
    Cup, the missing bread. Clever are the six

Handkerchiefs stitched to the size of a scarf
    And knotted at her throat. Poor is the thin

Coat, patched with cloth from the pockets
    She then sewed shut. Clever is the lipstick,

Petunia pink, she rubbed with a rag on her nails.
    Poor nails, yellow with cold. Posed

In a cape to hide her waist, her photograph
    Was clever. Poor then was what she called

The last bill twisted in her wallet. Letter
    After letter she was clever and more

Clever, for months she wrote a newspaperman
    Who liked her in the picture. The poor

Saved pounds of sugar, she traded them
    For stamps. He wanted a clever wife. She was poor

So he sent a ticket—now she could come to her wedding
    By train. Poor, the baby left with the nuns.

Because she is clever, on the platform to meet him
    She thinks, Be generous with your eyes. What is poor

Is what she sees. Cracks stop the station clock,
    Girls with candle grease to sell. Clever, poor,

Clever and poor, her husband, more nervous
    Than his picture, his shined shoes tied with twine.

They Lived Here

In a backwards accident,
Men cutting the old furnace
Out to make room for oil
Find the wedding band that
Slipped, in February
Nineteen twenty-four,
Down the heat vent and melted
To a coal. It was the coldest
Month of the year my mother
Was born, and The Captain
Sat quiet while his wife,
Her hands dressed in pie flour
And girlish without
The gold reminder, cried.
No one who was there
The night my grandmother
Lost the ring her husband
Brought her on *The Daisy*
From Brazil is still alive.
Not Fernstrom, the giant
Neighbor whose crowbar prised up
The iron grille, nor his
Wild sons Mack and Theo
Carrying an orchard ladder
Crusted with ice into
The parlor and fighting
Over who would climb
Down the galvanized duct.
Not Duchess, the terrier
Of wiry hair and almost
Human reason who patrolled
The hole's edge, and then,
Barking, led the men
To the cellar where they swear

She scratched at the belly
Of the coal box as if
She could smell gold. The Captain,
Singed by the lamp's hot
Kerosene as he hammered
To loosen the fuel bin's
Floor, is dead. Even
My grandmother, walking
Without coat or shawl
On the dark porch, her hand's
Misshapen fingers pressing
A snowball to her eyes,
Is gone. She told stories
Like this one. Mostly
I believe they were true,
Although she lied once
To my mother. She said
The Captain went singing,
Quick to heaven. My mother
Was small, there was a stroke.
She didn't know her father
Wandered out to Prince's
Stall and got the broken
Harness down to make Prince
Take the rusted bit, then
Gave him sugar for working
All day at the plough.
Her father used a pick
To clean each hoof, pulling
Loose the horseshoes over
Hooves he dug raw. A girl
That age would hardly
Remember a father at all,
So her mother lied.
He went quick to heaven,
Singing. But one thing
My mother saw was the barn step
As she fell, and a man

Who ran with her to the house.
Her eyes, she was cut, he was
Blurred red but she saw blue
Eyes and the sleeve of his coat
A black, rough blue. She knew
She hurt because he cried,
Running so fast she felt warm
In her blood. That must have been
Her father. He held her
Open head against the wool.

In Reserve

Your husband's laugh, a glass of grenadine.
    You greet the guests, steer coats onto your arms.
Ice rattles the kitchen: he's mixing drinks.
    You stand where you can keep an eye on him.
One measured glance at me, your face a smooth
    storm, and I know whatever I'd say—vague
murmurings in one of the kid's tidy rooms
    so you might open up—would be betrayal.
I compose myself. I'll not notice you
    notice already he has fixed the evening
on someone's out-of-town sister, neutral
    lovely blonde. Over her shoulder a green
scarf drifts like a bright apology he touches.
    —*I like this material. —Are you sure*
I'm not keeping you from your other guests?
    We'll all be drunk soon. Walk softly where starlings
have settled down in trees. They will wake
    to one pebble, the back door's silver click.

Why You Said It

for my sister Madeline

Then you've forgotten how we couldn't wait
for the bulldozers to raze that house
on Ridge Road. At the fresh edge
they'd butted into the woods,
the machines sat stalled for days, reluctant
to finish up the job. The goldfish pond
had already dried down to its beer cans
when our brothers started it, a few stones
to break the monotony of a picture window.
The provocation of the little flaws.
Kites of glass crunched under our feet
as we thumped through the empty rooms
like dice in a shoe box. The wallpaper
of smug begonias, one yank and it flowed
up the walls in long satisfying strips.
Wrapping ourselves in those paper boas,
we yelled, Goodbye, Good riddance,
Hit the road, Jack! and slammed the doors
harder, harder so cakes of plaster
slid through our hair. For an hour we rode
the bannister but couldn't bear how it
shuddered under our weight—
trying to make the best of things—
so we kicked it down the stairs.
And don't you remember the crowning touch?
We lassoed the chandelier with a scrounged necktie
and brought it down like a house of ice.

See how far back it goes? It's the tooth
I couldn't stop worrying till the roots
popped in my gums, the puncture in the cloth
that let you tear the lavender dress
into a cloud of lint. Once something starts

toward ruin, how good it feels
to help it go. That's why last night
when your lover hoisted his head
above yours—his scapegrace grin
a diffident shirt glimpsed above battlements—
something teetered in the balance,
scales in such airy equipoise
you couldn't help but tip them with a word.

The Next Child

I tell you she was here again last night.
While the wind scratched at the rafters
and we were caught up, fumbling
in the nightstand for diaphragm and jelly,
while Anna was giving her report from sleep,
rolling the heavy words through her crib slats
like cannonballs—our next child,
the child we will not have, rode in again,
rode in on the rain. Once again the chimney cap
was prized off and now lies pitched
in my newly bedded impatiens.
Again the tick tick in the fireplace,
the house filling with a reeking
gray muffle. And something fluttered
into the dogwood, its dark ribs bursting
the milkstars I'd set my sights on
into a thousand brown planets.
Brown planets? See what's happened to me?
When I look at the sky the sun
winks its swords at me. The telltale glint
through the trees mesmerized
the besieged at Dunsinane.
I don't know what it is, but it's not sky blue.

Anna races herself around and around
the breakfast table as if she could
catch herself coming and going.
Enough already, we tell her, such hunger
turned the tigers to a streak of butter
littered with parasols and purple shoes.
We've scattered this morning's paper
with the broken globes of oranges.
I twist a shard into the sunlight
to show her how it erupts, golden,

an atmosphere that flares brief as history,
then rains down sticky on our heads.
But even this bitter rind would be sweet
to that other child, snugged in the attic.
Light as fiberglass, she hangs by her feet
like a shut umbrella.

Dot

short for *daughter*—it was the best
they could do. Dad raised horses
near the Sweetwater,
selling to miners. February 1st,
three feet of snow and the cabin
burned down, though the lucky barn
was saved. The day I was born, Father
bedded Mother in the stallion's stall, moving
Old Bud in with a mare. Mother
once told me, what she remembered most
was the swish-swish of Bud rubbing his rump
against the wall next to her.

At six, I started Miss Betty's first grade.
Coming home: Mother on her hands and knees
scrubbing the pine plank floor. Grabbing
her side, she said, Dot, a glass of water.
I called my sister who told me to get
on the mule, fetch the neighbors a mile away.
I brought the water, most of it spilled—
I always wondered if that's why
she died. It's a sad thing, but
a mule cannot be hurried.

My brother married Miss Betty and they
took my baby brother as
mining-town life didn't suit Father's new wife.
After school, Stepmother waited
behind the door, coming at me
with a stick. Bloodied and torn, I had to
clean myself up, so I never
found out what I'd done wrong. She wasn't

all bad. A seamstress, she made me
the prettiest red dress,
tatted collar, sleeves trimmed in velveteen—
the only thing I dared to love.
Everyone at church said,
Isn't Dot the luckiest girl? One day Stepmother
grabbed my wrist and made me
watch as she scissored my little red dress like
chicken innards. All she said was: If you tell,
I'll drown you in the river. Ever since Mother died
I'd been terrified of water, something
about the glassful she never got and that
bucket of lye suds she'd used for scrubbing...

It was decided I should live with my sister
who had a weak heart like Mother and a little
blind hermaphrodite daughter whom
I took care of while her husband ran a trading post
where I also worked.
Sometimes I counted and wrapped
Winesaps which wintered
in the warehouse cellar, sized russets,
turned acorn squash.
Her husband's narrow face and scraggly beard
reminded me of a parsnip. He was always
trying to get me to himself, feeling
where my breasts would be.
At night I was afraid to sleep.
During the day my sister would say, I'm so tired, Dot,
won't you take these eggs to the mercantile?
I wouldn't. *He* was there.
My sister threw up her hands, complaining
to her husband who told me:
If you say a single word,
it'll kill her.

Didn't eat much, stayed thin so I could
slide between the warehouse boards whenever

he cornered me grading potatoes. The fact
that he carried two hundred pounds with only his parsnip
face about to slip between those planks was what
saved my bacon. For years afterward I dreamed
the noise of his feet climbing down the cellar ladder.
Seven rungs—that's how long I had to get away.

His assistant was twenty-four.
I was sixteen. He earned $3.50 a week. We never
let on except for stealing a kiss. Three dollars
for the marriage license, a dime for each
train ticket to Boise. I lost track of
the remaining thirty cents. All that mattered was
finally I had someone to love me.

My sister died, my brother-in-law was held
in high esteem—he took care of that
little hermaphrodite, who never spoke or grew,
until she was forty. Because of
those beatings, I've always been
shy and never able to hold
with public opinion.

Laura Soward, b. 1897

Midday, Too Hot for Chores

July 1878

Even sage hens were panting.
Belle Bishop and I dangled our feet
in a cooling bucket of well water while
sewing clothes for our corn husk dolls.
On the horizon, particles like a fine snow blew
across washboard sand and platinum
wheat grass. Sheep stampede, I said.
And Belle said, Corn silk
does not make good
doll hair. I told Belle wheat grass
would do better. Mother, who always
kept a keen eye on the heavens, came out
holding Baby Bessie. Since my sister
married last month, Mama looked
thin as a pea vine always wanting
a doorway to twine herself in.
I asked her who would I marry, and Belle
asked her who would she marry.
Mama stared at the dust veiling
the sun, her face puckered like apples
we made dolls from last March.
Every pot has his lid, she said, her last word
sliding into the hoof knock of an
Indian (was it?) riding at terrible speed
for this heat. Mama grabbed us girls,
slammed the door, bracing
it with the chopping block. Pushing
Belle and me under her and Papa's bed,
she hid baby in the pie safe, pulling
Father's Winchester from the wall.
In the underground dark Belle and I
splayed across a lumpy tow sack,
grainy particles grinding into

our knees, palms, scratching my cheek,
my tongue reaching to it. Outside a man
(a white man) shouted: While Owl's band!
Burned Pilot Rock and
heading this way! My tongue
clung to the sacking. Finally,
I'd found where Mama hid
the sugar.

Mrs. Bishop's Pilot Rock Chapeaux
and Notions Shop, 1882

stood across the dusty street from Sam's
Shade Tree Saloon. Once, during a holdup, bullets
whizzed through the door past the trimmer's chair where
Mama sat not five minutes before. That was the year of
the flood, when we had to pile hat trimmings on high
shelves and escape with our lives and Mama's
wool dress. "Count your blessings, Belle," Mama said,
pulling a cartwheel hat from lapping water.
"All your Kansas grandmother had was a wilted
sunbonnet—they buried her in it."
Merry widow hats, hats with tiny
crowns and short backs sticking out
a foot in front, hats no bigger than
the palm of your hand. How could we
save them all? Mama instructed: "Belle, when you
grow up always skewer your hat to the front
of your pompadour with a single pin, anything more
is excessive." I was only nine and could not swim and was not
allowed to play with the hair goods Mama was trying
to save: switches, rats, transformational braids—
the eleventh commandment:
Build up thy head size so thy hat has
somewhere to sit. Mrs. Webb's headwear?
The size of a saucer with a sharply turned edge,
fashioned from blue illusion, trimmed in
forget-me-knots, two ties knotted under the chin.
Dawn till dusk the day before Mama had sewn its lining,
her wagging arm reminded me of Mrs. Brokenhorn's
fly-chasing tail, back and forth, back and forth, stitching
an ecstasy of a black velvet bandeaux coyly
peeping through the brim. Two entire days
to shirr enough chiffon and all of it about to drown!
Hat shapes, hat stands, hat racks, threatened to float

away while the noise of rising water out-shouted
town gossip: The mayor's wife changed
trimmings so many times the straw wore out!
Mama put her hands to her temples every time
she thought of it. A boat-shaped black velvet model
trimmed in willow plume and bird of paradise,
a tiny import covered with artificial thistle;
the first New York headwear displayed in Pilot Rock.
Mama standing there in her black
wool dress, paper lining her leg-of-mutton sleeves; so puffed
up she had to turn sideways to fit through our door.
I began to cry. How would we save "Billy"
our sewing machine? Water in my shoes, my legs
shivered. Would anyone come to carry us out? What about
Mrs. Brokenhorn? I asked Mama if cows could swim.
"Be good and be happy to live in these times,"
she said, holding her skirt above the water line,
"when we have trimmed hats to wash
away the dust of everyday life."

In France They Turn to Stone When They Die

The old woman drowsed beneath an overhang of Orphan Annie hair. The blast of orange swirls and curlicues was blinding in the sun. Monsoon wondered how the old lady could sleep with all that brightness in her face.

His backside was going numb against the pavement. Blinking, he scooched sideways for an up-close look at her. Wasn't looking none too good. The old woman had the sort of face reminded you there was a skull behind it. Her skin was bluish-white, taffy-speckled. Her mouth looked like some kid had crayoned it in to fill the gap between the sharp points of her nose and chin.

"Baby," Monsoon crooned. "Ooh-ooh, baby."

The old woman opened her eyes and stared at him without expression. Her eyes were the straightforward blue of the larkspur spikes along his granny's fence back in Macon. His granny hadn't got no eyelashes, neither, at the end, no brows to speak of. Old ladies lasted long enough, they always got around to having a naked look.

"Fuck off." This one's voice, though, she sounded like a little girl, even when she got to cussing him out. "Fuck off," she said. "I mean it."

Monsoon smiled like he'd accomplished something. "Hey," he said.

"What do you want?" Her chin pointed at him like a finger.

"Want to eat you," Monsoon said. "Want to eat you up, babe." He grinned. A few of his teeth were missing. Those left were very white and looked like they'd been filed down to render him harmless.

"Uppity nigger," the old woman said.

"White bitch."

They smiled at each other like parties to an agreement. The street around them was empty of people, crowded with debris. Something as pure as sunlight a sin. The old woman, still smiling, shut her eyes. After a minute Monsoon did, too. "Lap you up like cream till you scream," he said.

"Load me up on the spuds," Monica said. "Forget about that green stuff."

The girl behind the steam table smiled. There was mist on her glasses. Monica wondered how she could see.

"Where are you going to get your vitamins?" the girl asked.

"You don't want to know," said Monica.

The girl, a student from some college, was always there on Thursdays, always asking questions. She wore loose khaki shorts, even now, in November. At twelve-thirty, when the line was shut down on the dot, she'd come out from behind the counter and wander from table to table, butting in, making people talk who didn't want to, interrupting those who did. Her name was Karen. Her legs reminded Monica of butterscotch pudding, thick and lumpy and yellowish. Every time Monica saw Karen's legs, she wanted to kick her in the shins.

A spoonful of instant mashed potatoes landed beside a slice of Spam that had a ring of pineapple and a cherry nailed to it with a toothpick.

"You can do better than that," Monica said.

Karen's smile dimmed. She dropped another dab of potatoes on the gray plastic plate. "All right?"

"Don't go overboard."

Monica pushed past a little kid in a Roger Rabbit T-shirt who had big eyes for the day-old doughnuts. All the ones with frosting were gone. At the end of the line, she snatched up three slices of dry white bread, slipping them into a pocket. Thursday nights, supper was in a church basement halfway across town. She might not feel like making the trip.

She was late because of falling asleep in the library, in the little room where they kept the magazines and a couple of almost-comfortable chairs. You weren't allowed to sleep in there. She should probably thank that biddy with the fuzzy blue hair for throwing her out. Otherwise she would have missed out on lunch today.

Monica stood by the end of the counter and looked around the room. The white cinder-block walls were painted with clouds and rainbows and flowers that looked like they had faces. The low ceiling and the pipes that ran across it were blue, as if they could fake the sky. As far as Monica could see, there was no room for her anywhere.

The tray was getting heavy and the straps of her backpack cut into her shoulders. A lot of people were finished, just sitting there taking up room. Bastards. Monica thought about sitting down right where she was and eating on the floor. Probably wouldn't get as far as swallowing the first bite, though. Make anything they call trouble, you weren't allowed back in for two weeks. Monica'd been put off limits more than once. They meant business. "The bastards," she said.

Her legs were swelled up but good today. She could feel the pain pushing up through the rest of her, like something getting ready to bust. Monica squeezed her eyes shut. *Gusher,* she thought. The word came back to her from a movie she saw once. It was in Texas and had Montgomery Clift in it. Monica pictured blood bursting up out of her head, black and thick, covering everything. Nobody who got anywhere near her would ever be able to wash it off.

Monica's arms had started trembling, when the tray's weight was suddenly lifted from them. Her eyes flashed open. She saw the food moving out of her reach. It looked better than it had when the girl was dishing it up.

"Come on, babe," Monsoon said. "Got you a sit-down."

"You," Monica said.

He kept walking.

Monica followed, trying to keep up with him. The throbbing in her ankles felt like sucking mud. "Who the hell do you think you are?"

"You got all day," Monsoon said over his shoulder, "maybe I tell you."

Monica spotted two empty chairs at a long plywood table near the back of the room. A tray with a half-eaten meal sat at one place. The other was empty.

"Think I'm about to eat with you," Monica said, "you got another think coming."

"Meaner you talk, the hotter I get, mama." Monsoon set down her tray and pulled out her chair. "Gon' wine and dine you."

Monica came to a halt, looking up at him. He was more than a foot taller than she was, snaky through the hips, wide as a garage door at the shoulders. She thought he was maybe forty, but it was impossible to tell in people who weren't white. He was too damn old, anyhow, to act like he did.

"I'll eat," Monica said. "But I ain't talking."

He grinned, his small white teeth flashing behind a beard like a cloud of black smoke. "Suits me," he said.

Monica struggled free of her red backpack and eased it to the floor. Her coat, a flare of shredding purple satin with nibbles of yellowed white fur at the collar and cuffs, fell heavily on top of it, the contents of its pockets clanking. She began peeling elbow-length black gloves from her bent fingers.

"Woo," Monsoon said, "take it *off!*"

Ignoring him, she plunked herself down on the metal chair. Her feet didn't touch the floor. Pale flesh puffed out over the tops of her blue bowling shoes like bread dough somebody forgot to punch down.

"You better not look at me, either," she said. "I'm armed."

He didn't know what got him started watching her, why lately it was starting to seem like a habit. She just tickled him sometimes. But mostly the old lady was like a bad accident, Monsoon thought. You didn't want to look but couldn't seem to stop your-self.

They'd both been on the street for a few years now, Monsoon since the old VA hospital shut down, Monica since the rooming house on Diversey burned up. Not that this was the first time for either of them on the street. Just the longest. And maybe the last, the way things were looking. Monsoon made out all right. Seemed like maybe the old lady was wearing down, though.

Monica had always been around somewhere, on the edges of things, as far back as he could remember. She wouldn't always have been old, of course, but his memory hadn't kept any other pictures of her.

"What do you want from me?" she'd ask him sometimes when

she caught him staring at her. "What the hell are you after?"

"Want to sniff your drawers," Monsoon would tell her. "Find out is white meat as sweet as they say."

The more impervious the old woman seemed, the harder Monsoon tried to get under her skin. She brought out his poetic streak. "Want to lick your knickers," he said. "Take a spin through your skin . . . won't never let me out once you get me in."

Monica just gave him a jaded look. "You're no James Whitcomb Riley, bub," she said.

Monsoon didn't understand more than a tenth what she talked about. Hello and goodbye, please and thank you, didn't exist in her language. Sometimes when Monsoon laid hold of a bottle, he'd share it with her. The old lady favored apricot brandy and gin, but she'd drink anything, long as she wasn't expected to show gratitude for it.

One spring night—must have been back in May, it wasn't really warm yet—they'd gnawed on sweet-and-sour baby sparerib bones in the alley behind Cafe Polynesia, meanwhile polishing off a whole fifth of peppermint schnapps Monsoon had risked his neck to come by. The old dude who kept the package store over by the Greyhound had a gun down under the counter. Wasn't nobody didn't know it since the Preston boy got blown away for a pint of Ron Rico and a couple Slim Jims.

"Stuff tastes like Colgate," Monica said.

"Ain't nobody making you imbibe, old woman."

" 'Imbibe'?" The old lady had a laugh like a maggoty old myna bird he'd seen in a whorehouse in Bangkok, sound to make a man's cock keel over limp as collards.

"Means *drink*." Monsoon was haughty.

"I know what it means," said Monica. "What I don't know is where you get off sounding so uppish." She tossed back another mouthful before passing the bottle back to him. "Pegged you for a phony the first time I saw you."

"Nothin' phony 'bout me," said Monsoon. "Not like, say, that hair you wearin'."

The old woman grinned. "How about your *name*?" She sniffed. "Monsoon. Gimme a break."

"They give it to me in the army," he said. "Means a storm."

"Somebody say I needed an interpreter?" She snatched the bottle and took a long swallow. "Ferocious like a storm, huh? Is that what I'm supposed to think?"

"Hot and wet and—" He licked his lips and smiled dirty. "Liable to start up out of nowhere and go on for weeks."

The old lady shrugged. "I seen some real storms," she said.

Monsoon looked her over. "I can see that," he said.

At dawn, behind a dumpster smelling of tropical fruits and rotting fish, they'd thrown up together. Monsoon hardly remembered that part, though, except he'd lost his taste for peppermint schnapps since then. What came back to him afterwards, locked onto his mind, was how the old lady, once she got oiled, had jabbered on through the chilliest part of the night, telling him in a dreamy voice about some old church outside of Paris where the corpses of kings and queens were just lying right there where you could see them.

Monsoon had run into a few corpses himself. The Mekong Delta was full of them. But in a church, left to lie for more than a hundred years and nobody even burying them?

Their fingers were as long and tapered as silver dinner knives, Monica said. And their faces looked snooty, like they were turning up their noses at heaven.

"Must stink in there," Monsoon said. "All them dead carcasses."

Monica shook her head.

"Must." Monsoon was definite. "And flies . . ."

"In France they turn to stone when they die." The old woman laughed. If it was a joke, Monsoon didn't get it.

"And maggots," he said. "Shit."

Monica just kept laughing.

Her daddy had been some Frenchie stonecutter, she said, who made marble angels and swans and lambs to decorate gardens and graves. They lived up north, in Vermont. When Monica was sixteen, her mama died in a mill fire. Her daddy took it in his mind to sell the house and use the money to take his one and only child to see the dead kings and queens in the church where he got baptized when he was just a week old, and they went on a big boat.

"I was sick the whole way," Monica said. "My father just stood out on the deck and stared at the sea, never said a word. The waves got as big as those high-rises over there." She nodded toward State Street. "He looked like a statue," she said. "I saw it coming."

"What?"

"Just never you mind," she said.

Monsoon was skeptical. "You really been to Paris, France?"

Monica nodded. Her eyes were an ocean away.

"San Denny," she called the place, or something like that. "I tell you, death don't make a dent," she said.

"I know what you mean," Monsoon said after a while. He wanted to tell the old lady about the times he'd walked away from it himself, but she'd gone fast asleep in the crook of his arm by then.

When he was sure she was out, Monsoon touched her hair. It reminded him of something you'd scour out pots with. With the lipstick gone, her mouth was just a little round opening. Her lips made a soft popping sound that sent a sour minty smell up around his face.

Before long, Monsoon, his back propped against the restaurant's concrete back stoop, dozed off, too. He dreamed about the church he'd never seen and could hardly believe in. The dead kings and queens and even Jesus on his cross were all turned to stone. When he woke up, Monica was gone. His bottle was bonedry, and the sky in the east, yellowish and full of long stringy clouds, looked like egg drop soup.

Been on top of things, Monsoon thought, woulda seen trouble coming and headed it off. Like it was, though, too busy working on getting a rise out of the old woman. So it was easy for Darnelle to come sneaking up behind, the loony shine in her eyes like usual, only brighter. Picking pink gristle out his teeth and talking dirty left them both, him and the old lady, wide-open.

"Gon' bury my nose in your panty hose," was what he was saying, a new one he'd been saving up for her. "Stroke your leg till you beg."

Monica, her mouth crammed full of white stuff, was paying him no mind.

"Mama in for a treat 'cause I'm a—"

Darnelle swooped down like a flighty blackbird, all flap and claw and cackle. Next thing he knew, the old lady was laid out flat on the floor, food and spit running down her chin and her legs splayed out pale and puffy and advertising her serious need of some underwear.

Seemed, though, like Monica didn't know what was left to showing, her dress bunched up at her waist that way. Her hands had no thought but to cover her head. Meanwhile, crazy Darnelle Featherstone's dancing out the door toting Monica's wig like Salome with John the Baptist's head on a plate, a sight so unreal that it maybe explained why nobody even tried to stop her. She wasn't right in the head, Darnelle. Wasn't nobody didn't know it. Monsoon knew it better than most.

Monica wasn't getting up.

"You all right, mama?" Monsoon said.

What come from her mouth hadn't a thing to do with words. The soft, weak sounds were worse than screaming. They made heads turn away. Folks gave up eating. Even Monsoon, for a second, had to close his eyes.

When he got himself together enough to open them again, Monica was still on the floor, all nakedness below and ruin above, her head like an egg in the nest of her small freckled hands.

Monsoon knelt down beside her, yanked down her skirt. "Let's fix you up," he said. With his bare fingers, he wiped the food and spit from her face, rubbed his hands on his pants.

"Come on." He stood up slowly, then reached down to pull her up.

The terrible soft sounds kept leaking from her mouth, her hands kept hold of her skull. A few wisps of hair, thin and white as spider webs, were pasted to her scalp.

Leaning down, Monsoon grasped Monica under the arms and lifted her to her feet. There was hardly any weight to her. She went silent, pressing her lips together. Her eyes like nobody's home.

"We'll see to her, thank you." The steely-eyed sister in charge was all of a sudden in his face, that nosy Karen behind her. Making hushing sounds, they enclosed the old lady like brackets and led her away. She looked like a tiny child between them. They vanished into the corridor behind a fire door that said "Staff Only."

When Monica didn't return after more than half an hour, Monsoon got up to go. The dining hall was empty, the tables cleared and scrubbed down. Clanking pans and rushing water made a racket in the kitchen. The hot room smelled of Lysol and over-cooked food.

Before he went out to the street, Monsoon picked up the old woman's things and placed them on the table. The backpack was heavy. Seemed like even the thready coat packed more heft than she did.

He didn't see her at the soup kitchen, or anywhere, for four days. Not that he was actually looking for her, but the old lady wasn't anywhere.

After it snowed on Sunday night, though, Monsoon couldn't stop thinking about that crazy purple coat of hers. Like something Billie Holiday might have been wearing to jump from a limo to the Cotton Club's stage door. Only that would have been fifty years ago, when the coat was new. And not in winter, either. Empty out them big pockets, that rag wouldn't add up to a pound on a cheating butcherman's scale.

He knew everywhere to look. Wasn't a warm spot or dark corner in the city Monsoon hadn't ducked into himself a time or two. But he didn't know a soul to ask. It dawned on him now what a loner the old lady was. He'd never seen her hanging out with nobody. Fact was, he might be about the only one she ever talked with, if you could call that talking.

Thing was, she'd need to eat. And get in and out of the nights, now it was down under freezing. There was only so many places. She wasn't showing up at none of them.

Monday nights, the Salvation Army dished out chili at the shelter in the old armory. The chili, lukewarm and gluey, without a bit of spice or meat in it, was something he'd look forward to about as much as withdrawal. Rather go hungry Monday evening than pass Tuesday morning in the bus station lavatory with the trots. Monsoon figured he'd swing by the armory, though, in case the old lady wandered in. She had a cast-iron stomach. Maybe he could choke down a cup of their stewed coffee while he checked things out.

Monica wasn't there. But Darnelle Featherstone, crazy bitch, was. Monsoon saw her traipsing through the line, had on red and white knee socks like one of Santy's elves with them stiletto-heel pumps she been wearing till they got ground down to bitty stumps. The old lady's hair was hanging from Darnelle's belt loop like a scalp on some damn Injun warrior.

Monsoon dawdled back by the coat rack, making himself scarce until Darnelle sat down on a wooden bench along the wall. He let her get a big mouthful half-chewed before he got the jump on her. The wig came off her belt with a ripping sound.

"Ought to kill you," he said.

He expected her to let loose with a yell. Darnelle was famous for that. Every couple months she'd clear a place out—the soup kitchen or bus terminal, a schoolyard, even a church, she didn't care—with her haint hollering that made your heart stop and your eardrums hope to hell you were dying.

But she must have been losing steam, Darnelle, or on something. She just looked up at Monsoon with those how-now-brown-cow eyes and kept right on eating.

Monsoon bent down, bringing his face right next to hers. "See you fuck with that lady...see you fuck with *anybody* that way again," he said, "I will seriously mess with you."

Darnelle laughed, her teeth all stuck with them mashed brown beans. "Been hopin' you do somethin' to me, baby. It's a while now, ain't it?"

Monsoon, looking at her, felt sick. He had done, once. Darnelle never let him forget it. High as the moon and crazier than she was, back then. She said he was her baby's daddy, even though the little girl got born two, three years after that one sorry night.

Monsoon crushed Monica's wig and shoved his fist into his pocket. Darnelle's smile was sweet, loose like her mind.

"How you getting on?" Monsoon said after a moment. "How's Jamiel?"

"She missing her poppy." Darnelle licked her teeth, then smiled again. She looked almost like the fine young thing she used to be, running the streets with Monsoon's baby sister when he had one.

"She—what—four now, Jamiel?"

Darnelle blinked. "Six," she said. "Ought to come round and see her."

"She with you now?" The little girl had been, so far as he knew, in foster homes since she was a year old.

Darnelle's placid brown eyes went hazy. She mumbled something, her mouth full again.

"Say what?"

She was staring across the room at a long span of empty bench. The chili wasn't selling too good. There weren't twenty people in the huge cold room.

"Say I got pitchers," Darnelle said. "Come by and see her, all right?"

Monsoon sighed. "Maybe I do that," he said.

Darnelle hunched over her bowl, her eyes half-closed. Her jaw muscles were twitching up and down. Monsoon couldn't tell if she was chewing or praying or shivering.

"You take care now, Darnelle," he said. "Hear?"

She started humming "Here Comes the Sun."

Monsoon shoved his hands deep into his pockets as he headed out into the cold. The old lady's wig felt cool and shapeless and stiff, like something dead at the side of a lonely road.

Nothing he tried to find her turned up a clue. The old lady didn't leave tracks. When he finally got mad and gave up looking, Monsoon nearly tripped over her.

At first he thought she was dead. The old lady was laid out on a marble slab at the foot of a side altar in the little Catholic church on Market Street. Her backpack was shoved under her head like a lumpy pillow, her coat spread over her. A painted statue of Mary and the Baby Jesus was backed into a carved hollow above the little altar, a bank of stubby candles in red shot glasses burning below. Their light made Monica's small, sharp profile look like marble, pink as dawn and veined with blue.

A church would have been the last place he'd think of to look for her. He wouldn't have gone in himself if the night hadn't been so damn cold and the church the first place he saw that he could get inside. St. Martin de Porres was the only church in the whole city that kept open all night now.

When the council had passed a law that all churches had to be locked after dark except with services going on, Father Mack, the pastor, raised holy hell. The homeless had to have someplace to go, he said. The city got all heated up over it. Hazard, they said. Public nuisance, they said. When Father Mack and St. Martin's got a judge to see things right, the council retaliated by yanking all the benches out of Buchanan Park.

Nobody took much advantage of the church, for all of that. It was dark and damp and barely heated. From spring to fall, though, the park benches had been sort of like a club. Folks felt safe there, clustered under the big amber lights. Sometimes a band got going. Now everybody was on their own.

Two old bums in one raggedy sleeping bag were filling the church vestibule with snores and the smell of cheap bourbon. Monsoon nearly stepped on them on his way in. Not that they'd likely notice. The candles drew him up front to the side altar. From a distance their pale red light looked warm.

The toes of his boots stopped only a few feet short of the old woman. Monsoon froze for a moment. Her chest didn't seem to be moving.

He dropped to his knees and lowered his cheek near her mouth. Her lips were just slightly parted. He felt the fever from her skin before her breath touched his cheek. "Oh shit," he said.

Her eyes, purplish-black in the candlelight, gave away no surprise or alarm. She just looked at him. "You again," she said.

Her hands were clasped on her chest, outside the covering of her coat. She lifted them slowly and touched her head, her palms over her ears, her fingers like claws. When she felt the black knit cap, she pulled it down more snugly, then her hands dropped away. "What the fuck you want?"

Monsoon tried to come up with reason or rhyme, but he'd lost the taste for sass. Heat radiated from her scrawny body, washing up over his knees and thighs like a warm tide, rising up to his belly, his chest, as he knelt over her.

"Where you been, mama?"

"Around." Monica struggled to sit up.

"Been lonesome for you."

She turned and looked at the statue of Mary and the Child. "What a crock," she said.

"Brought you something."

Her eyes brightened a little. "To drink?"

"Better." Monsoon reached into his pocket and pulled out the wig. The curls had gone flat and tangled. He tried to fluff it up a little before passing it to her.

She dropped the wig on the altar without a glance. "You got anything to eat?"

"You want the prime rib or the turkey?" Monsoon grinned. "Woulda brought ribs but they kinda messy."

"You're a real hoot," Monica said. "You know it?" She lay back down and pulled her coat up to her chin, folding her arms under it.

"Look like a damn mummy," Monsoon said.

She didn't answer him. Her legs, exposed to the knee, were bare, and one was badly ulcerated, a festering overblown rose above her ankle.

"Under the weather, ain't you?" Monsoon slipped off his army jacket and covered her legs.

She kicked at the jacket, and it flew off the marble step and landed in the darkness below them. "I'm all right."

"Oh, yeah," Monsoon said. "Can see you fine."

She shut her eyes.

"Ought to take what you can get," Monsoon said gently. "If it's all somebody got to give you."

Her eyes flashed open. "You can go to hell," she said. Then her eyelids lowered again, and she pressed her lips together until her mouth disappeared into itself.

"Remind me of a' aspirin," he said. "Bitty old white thing, all hard and sour."

The old woman stayed locked in behind her eyes.

Monsoon, still kneeling, dropped his butt to the floor beside her. The marble was cold and slick as ice. "Okay," he said. "That's how you want to be."

After a time his own eyes grew heavy. He reached down below the step, found his jacket, and laid it over her legs again. Then he sidled closer to the heat of her and closed his eyes.

"And you can just stop looking at me, too," Monica said.

Monsoon laughed softly. "You carrying again?"

She was staring at the statue. Mary's head was bent in what

might have been modesty or sorrow or shame. But the Child's eyes, penetrating, full of light, seemed to be taking in everything—the old lady, Monsoon, the sleeping bums and the empty pews, the small spill of light and the infinite darkness beyond it.

"I can see perfect in the dark," she said. "Always could."

Monsoon wrapped his arms around himself and rested his forehead on his knees. "Me, too," he said.

"We shoulda been spies."

"Right," Monsoon said. "But which side?"

The old woman's hands crept out from under the coat and stroked a snip of pale fur. Her breathing whistled like the wind.

"Overboard in a storm on the way home," she said.

He figured she was talking in her sleep. Monsoon had heard the courthouse clock strike three—seemed like hours ago, but it hadn't chimed four yet. Though he was far from sleep himself, he wasn't really awake, either. The old lady's breathing had got to sounding tough and tangled now, like weeds she couldn't get through.

"The captain tore up the letter. If it was an accident, I'd get some money, he said. The little bits of white paper flew up in the air, and I never saw them touch the water."

Without raising his head, Monsoon reached out to touch her face. His fingers were too cold to tell if she was really getting hotter. Seemed like, though. "Ssh," he said. "Get back to sleep now."

"The angels' heads were always bent down," she said. "Their wings kept folded up tight."

"All right," Monsoon said. "Ssh."

"For a long time I remembered that like something that only happened after she burned up. You know?"

"Uh-huh." Monsoon's palm smoothed her forehead. "You hush now."

"But when I got older than him, which was soon, I knew he was always sad." She sighed. "Always. Even the garden angels with the sun all over them made me cry. You couldn't see it, but all the wings were broken."

"It's okay," Monsoon whispered.

"Some people are an accident before they even get born." She tossed her head, and his hand slipped from his brow. "You think I'm dreaming," she said bitterly. "You're making a big mistake if you think I don't know the difference."

Monsoon lifted his head from his knees. The old lady's eyes were wide-open, intent on his face.

"No," Monsoon said. "You're not dreaming."

After a moment, she nodded.

"Probably ought to be gettin' some rest, though," he said.

She laughed hoarsely. "Nod out now I'll miss the best part." She coughed, her body going rigid. The will she exerted to stop was like another person between them. When her body finally went lax, Monsoon, alone with her, felt frightened.

Her eyes were watering. Monsoon wiped them with the cuff of his sweatshirt.

"Listen, you," Monica said. "I can handle it."

"Never said you couldn't."

She smiled. "For a long time I thought I knew what I was waiting for. Exactly."

He waited.

"The fucking angels would rear up their heads like wild horses," she said. "Christ."

"Ain't nothing like that," Monsoon said.

"It's like the kings and queens," she said. "All stone and stillness."

Her voice had grown weak. She was shivering.

"Got to warm you up," Monsoon said.

"For what?" Her laugh was strangled by coughing.

"Never mind." Monsoon unknotted himself, stretching his arms and legs. Then, moving slowly, he inched down beside her.

"Don't," she whispered. "That's close enough."

"Okay." He slipped an arm under her neck, lifted her head from the backpack, and cradled it in the crook of his arm.

"You should have seen me." Her breath wreathed his face, bitter and steamy.

Monsoon drew her closer. "I reckon," he said.

"He put my face on every damn one of those angels." Her eyes brimmed and shimmered. "I saw myself everywhere," she said.

With surprising strength and quickness, Monica grabbed the shoulders of her coat and flipped it up into the air. Her pockets were empty now, had to be. The purple satin sailed, spreading out wide, hanging above them for a moment. Then it floated down again and enfolded them both inside it.

"I want you to get out of here," Monica said.

"It's freezing." Monsoon tightened his hold on her. "Long ways to morning."

She wrenched her head around and glared at him. "Fuck morning," she said.

She didn't talk for a long while after that, but Monsoon knew she wasn't sleeping. Her breathing was too labored, her body tight. The clock chimed four. She stayed close, letting him keep hold of her, but slanting her face away. He wondered if she saw the statue. Monsoon kept trying not to look at it.

The old woman let the echo of the fifth chime fade away before she rolled away from him. "Get going," she said. "I mean it." Her voice was firm and clear.

"No way."

She moved farther away, widening the chilly space between them. Monsoon could have held on, but he let her go. She didn't have much stamina. He wanted to fight fair.

"Go?" he said. "Why should I?"

She turned her back to him. "Because I'm telling you to," she said.

Monsoon sat up and rubbed his eyes. Still nothing but blackness to the church. "It's almost daybreak," he said. "We get some breakfast in you and—"

"Get the fuck out of here." She rolled onto her back and stared up at him.

It seemed like he was caught in her eyes forever. Her cap had fallen off and lay beside her on the floor in a pool of reddish light. Her head was nothing but a skull.

"Just wait, all right?" he said. "Hold on."

"I been waiting all my life," she said.

Monsoon smiled. "Think you can do a number on me, old woman?"

"Do anything I want," she said. "I'm armed."

In the back of the church one of the old men moaned in his sleep, then began to snore again. Monsoon stared at Monica. Her eyes, fixed on the statue, looked like polished dark stones. He looked up. For the first time Monsoon noticed that the Child held something round and gold with a little cross on the top of it.

"Please," Monica said.

The globe, gleaming a dull orange in the candlelight, looked too large, too heavy for the infant's hand. Monsoon sucked in his breath. Finally, he nodded. "Your call," he said.

"Thank you," the old woman said.

When he nodded again, his head felt like an impossible burden for his neck, and his shoulders ached.

Monsoon stood up slowly, easing his way back into his cramped limbs, his numb feet.

"Don't forget your jacket."

"You keep it."

"What the hell would I want with something like that?"

"Right." He picked up the jacket and put it on.

"See you," Monica said.

Monsoon hesitated. "What if you change your mind?" he said.

The old woman's laugh, short and sharp, pierced the silence like the cry of a frenzied bird.

The dark seemed bottomless. Monsoon stepped off the altar. One hand raised, he turned around and reached back toward the light, as if its frail radiance could steady him.

The old woman's profile was stony and white. His arm dropped to his side. "Be seeing you," he said.

Keeping his eyes on her, Monsoon backed into the dark. The blackness seemed to stretch at least as far above as it did below.

Smugglers

By folding his legs so that his feet touched his thighs, Matt was able to completely immerse himself in hot water—water he had paid for shilling by shilling, dropping small English coins into a rusted metal box one by one to keep the water flowing until the bathtub was full. The tiny washroom was freezing and filled with roiling white mist. Matt held his breath until his chest began to hurt, and then he popped his head above the surface just long enough to grab some air before sliding back under. It was three o'clock in the morning.

A half hour ago, he had been fucking Janice. She was wiped out and crazy on some lunatic assortment of pills and coke and grass, and she had literally jumped on him and torn off his shirt and bit his shoulder. Janice was fifteen. He hadn't wanted sex, but there was no way to deny her. When he came, she was already asleep. He rolled off her and closed his eyes, and then—it seemed to happen instantly—he was dreaming. Uncle Mike, his father's brother, strode toward him in an open, empty place, no surroundings really, just his uncle taking a few steps toward him. He was dressed immaculately in white, like a movie version of a Southern plantation owner, a crisp white suit tailored to his portly body. He wore a white, brimmed hat, and a white vest with a watch's gold chain dangling stylishly from a vest pocket. His hands were clasped in front of him, and he said, "Matt. You'll never make it." Then there was a noise and the dream dissolved and Matt woke up with the image of his uncle vivid in his mind, his uncle who in reality was a ragged-looking, thin man with tattoos who always wore wrinkled clothes and who, his family guessed, had never run a comb through his long, greasy hair.

Someone had been knocking on the door: that was the noise that woke him. The clock on the nightstand said 2:46 a.m. He had rolled off Janice at 2:30. The knock came again, three times, a little louder, but still soft, as if the knocker had doubts about waking him so late at night. When he fully realized there was someone at the door, he sat up straight, and his heart took off like a sprinter. His apartment consisted of a single room with a bed; a gas fireplace, which also worked by feeding coins into a meter; and a table and chair that served as a desk and an eating area. He turned on the nightstand light and checked the room. The cocaine was hidden, wrapped in aluminum foil inside his guitar case under the bed. A package of condoms sat in the middle of the table, beside a pair of airline tickets. He tossed the condoms and the tickets out of sight before answering the door. For a moment he had considered flushing the drugs down the toilet, but even half asleep he realized the bobbies wouldn't be knocking so tentatively.

It turned out to be his landlady with a telegram from home. "It's urgent," she had said, her hair in curlers, her heavy body wrapped tightly in a wrinkled blue robe. "It's from the States." Matt thanked her and she walked away quickly, as if embarrassed. The telegram read: *Uncle Mike had heart attack. Died Tuesday morning. Wake Wednesday and Thursday. Funeral on Friday. Please come home for funeral. Please.* It was from his mother, and when he read it, sitting on the edge of his bed, he got suddenly lightheaded. He was twenty-two, and he hadn't been home in more than a year. The words his uncle had spoken in the dream came back to him as if through an amplifier: "Matt. You'll never make it." His legs and arms began to shake. In the morning, with Janice, he was supposed to smuggle cocaine into Paris. Janice had done it many times. They were to wrap the cocaine inside condoms and swallow them just before the flight. When they got to Paris, they'd take a laxative, and the condoms would come out, the cocaine safe inside. He needed the money, and he had flirted with Janice and cajoled her and insinuated himself into her favor, and then he had started sleeping with her, a crazy, fifteen-year-old, lost little rich girl—all so that she would let him in on her deal. And now he was sure he would never make it. His uncle had come back from the dead to tell him. The flight would take too long and the latex would break down in his stomach and the massive dose of cocaine would kill him.

Water clung to Matt's skin as he climbed out of the bathtub.

When he saw himself in the full-length mirror on the back of the bathroom door, he was streaming clouds of mist. He dressed quickly, putting on heavy combat boots and jeans and a torn flannel shirt over a union suit that needed washing. Back in his room, the clothes that Janice had picked out for him, the cordovan loafers and khaki pants, the light-blue shirt with the button-down collar, and the London Fog overcoat—they lay neatly over the back of a chair, pressed and ready for the trip. Janice was sleeping on her side with her knees pulled up to her chest and her hands between her legs. Nights, out in the clubs, she looked like a teenage Shirley Temple gone bad, in torn blue jeans and a leather jacket, with a lingerie model's body and a little girl's face, a bad little girl. Asleep, she looked almost innocent, almost like a baby—but still wild, a wild innocence, even asleep, the way her wavy blond hair curled and tangled around plump cheeks and big eyes. In the morning she would scrub herself pink and pull her hair back into a ponytail before dressing up in a knee-length skirt and schoolgirl white shoes. That was her outfit for the Paris run.

Last time, Matt had helped her slide the condoms down her throat. She didn't need him to help, but there was something perversely erotic about it, pushing the cocaine-stuffed condoms down her throat while she sat on the floor by the bed, her head tilted all the way back and her eyes glittering with something that looked to Matt like craziness. Afterwards they had sex. Without asking, she had knelt by the bed, with her stomach on the mattress, and Matt had pulled up the knee-length skirt and pulled down the white cotton panties, and when he looked at her, he saw that she was laughing quietly to herself, as if amused by his predictability—as if she knew the whole scene would turn him on because he was a man and she was amused that she was right about him, that she had him pegged. When he finished, Matt had felt frightened. He had felt frightened and uneasy for days.

He pulled his guitar case out from under the bed and unlocked it with a small key he kept on a chain around his neck. He opened it carefully, holding each of the metal snaps as he pulled them up one by one. Inside the case, his guitar nestled snugly against a plush red lining. The polished blond wood of the soundboard reflected the red and blue flames from the gas fireplace, and the hand-carved hummingbird on the pick guard appeared to move in the wavering firelight. Matt lifted the guitar and removed his wallet from a small compartment under the neck. He had two five-pound notes folded up neatly next to his long-expired visa. He put the wallet in the back pocket of his jeans, locked up the guitar case, and slid it back under the bed.

Once on the street, he started for Stevie's apartment. Stevie sang for The Flesh Puppets, a band Matt had played with up until a couple of months ago. Matt had quit because he wanted Stevie for himself, and she wanted to do what she wanted, which included sleeping with women. After a few months, he realized anyway that her relationship with him was mostly for show. Really, it was other women that she wanted, lots of other women. So he left. But now, when he needed someone to talk with, someone to tell what had happened, to tell about his dream, he couldn't imagine who else but Stevie. Who else on the planet? He was twenty-two, and there had been three women in his life, excluding his mother. There was Cathy from home, from Wisconsin, whom he had started dating in ninth grade and gone out with at least once a week up until the time he shocked everyone and bought the charter ticket to London. But he had never really been able to talk to Cathy. He might tell her about his dream, and she would listen—but she would be uncomfortable. She would feel like he was turning the tables on her. Cathy was supposed to talk. He was supposed to listen. Then there was Janice, but her communication, with him, anyway, was mostly physical. That left only Stevie, and so Matt was headed for her building, which was only a short walk from his. With Stevie, the time of night wouldn't be a problem.

When he arrived at her apartment, he found the door half-open. A chokingly sweet haze of incense wafted into the hallway. Matt pushed the door open and found Richie and Dave sitting on the kitchen floor looking back at him with guitars in their laps.

"American Pie," Richie said, a clear note of relief in his voice.

"We been gettin' ripped off by the local scags," Dave said.

Richie opened a cabinet door under the sink and pulled out an ashtray with a couple of half-smoked joints. He placed the ashtray on the floor between him and Dave, and took a long drag off a joint. "We heard you coming up the stairs," he said, his voice high.

Matt said, "I'm looking for Stevie."

"There's a surprise," Richie said.

Dave pointed down the hall toward Stevie's bedroom. "She ain't alone, mate."

Matt said, "Is she ever?"

Dave turned back to his guitar. "Not often," he said softly, and he played a few chords and then looked up to Richie, who began to play along with him.

Matt followed the dimly lit corridor to Stevie's room. He stopped in front of the hanging beads that served as a door. The room behind the beads was lit by a single red candle on a curtainless window ledge, and drippings from the castle-shaped candle spilled over the ledge and down the wall to the baseboards. There was no real furniture in the room, only a mattress on the floor and some cardboard boxes spread around to serve as dressers and drawers. In the candlelight, Matt could see Stevie sitting up on her mattress, a sheet held over her breasts, her back against the wall, smoking a cigarette and looking at him through the bead curtain. She was a small woman, sylphlike in her movements, offstage; but when she sang, onstage, she moved in jerks, as if some great electric current regularly jolted her: first she'd be singing motionless, limp as the dead, then she'd suddenly fly in spasms around the stage, her arms and legs everywhere, as if she had lost her mind and all control of her body, and the music had possessed her, as if she'd suddenly gone crazy—and usually the audience went crazy with her. Matt hesitated on his side of the curtain. He could see another figure curled up beside Stevie on the mattress.

"My, my, hm hmm hmm," Stevie sang softly. "You just want to watch?"

"Watch what?" Matt parted the bead curtain and stepped into the room.

Stevie pulled back the covers on the girl sleeping next to her. She was young and smooth-skinned, her body sleek as an athlete's.

"Beautiful," Matt said.

She touched the sleeping girl's hair gently. "You want to join us?" she asked. "She'd be up for it. She's into good-looking men."

Matt sat on the floor beside Stevie. "Maybe," he said. He had tried that once before, sleeping with Stevie and one of her pick-ups. It had been strange in the beginning, in bed with two women, and even stranger at the end, when it was over, Stevie and her girl asleep cuddled into each other, and him on his side of the bed, alone. He felt like a sexual accessory. And he had been frightened, a kind of deep, unnameable anxiety shaking him up, keeping him from sleeping. In the morning, when he had told Stevie he wouldn't do it again, she had been disappointed. But now, with Stevie's offer, he could feel his blood moving. "I need to talk to you," he said. "Something incredible just happened."

"What?" She put out her cigarette and leaned toward him. Her interest was apparent in her eyes, which took on a vibrant, glittery quality when she was excited. "Really?"

Matt told her about his dream and the telegram.

"Was he sick?" Stevie asked. "Could you have known?"

"He wasn't old. He wasn't sick." Matt touched his forehead as if checking for a fever. "It's blowing me away."

Stevie grinned. She seemed pleased, as if something she already knew was now being revealed to Matt, something that would make them closer when they both knew. "You never saw him dressed like that? An old picture or something?"

"He was a slob. That's the last way—"

Stevie said, "Then you know it was real."

"But I need to know what it means."

Stevie slid down on the mattress and propped her head up on one hand. The sheet fell loosely over her breasts. "You want everything wrapped up," she said. "That's why we could never work."

Matt said, "What are you talking about?"

"It happened. It's a mystery."

"It doesn't make you ask questions? Like, Where's he going? How come he was dressed like that? What happens when you die?"

She touched Matt's knee. "I'm not into controlling things. I'm into the music of it."

Matt closed his eyes and let his chin drop to his chest. He wanted silence for a moment. He wanted to think. Stevie and Richie and Dave—they thought of him as an innocent, as a boy. They called him American Pie, or Apple Pie, even though he smoked dope with them, and played with them, and slept with Stevie: no matter what he did, it didn't seem to change their perception of him. Partly, it was the way he looked. He had a round, boyish face that made him look even younger than he was, young enough that no one ever questioned him hanging around with a fifteen-year-old girl; and he had the straight, white teeth and the healthy skin of a milk-fed, well-cared-for child. He looked like a six-foot two-inch baseball player from Iowa—which is exactly what he had been in high school, except he was from Wisconsin. But he was twenty-two now, and he wanted something different. He wasn't sure what Stevie meant about *controlling things,* or *the music of it,* but he wasn't going to ask. "Me, too," he said. "I'm into the music of it, too, but—"

"What about what he said?" Stevie interrupted. "What do you think *that* means?"

"That's the scary part." The sheet over Stevie had drifted down, revealing most of her breasts and her back. Matt could feel his breath catching in his throat when he spoke. "Can I lie next to you?" he asked. "Would that be all right?"

Stevie lifted the sheet, inviting him to crawl in next to her. Matt looked at her for a long moment, taking in her body, the swellings and curves, the light and dark places. Then he lay down next to her, facing her, and she covered them both with the sheet. Behind Stevie, the other woman stirred and then sat up and looked, surprised, at Matt. "What's this?" she said, not bothering to cover herself up, an edge of anger in her voice.

"He's a friend," Stevie said, without turning around. "We're talking."

The woman seemed to think about this for a moment. Then she smiled and said, as if excusing her momentary anger, "I'm still asleep," and she cuddled up into Stevie, wrapping her arms around her chest and snuggling against her.

"What's the scary part?" Stevie said. "Just what exactly did he say?"

"What I told you. He said I'm not going to make it. He took, like, two steps toward me, and he had this concerned, like, sad look on his face, and he goes, 'Matt, you'll never make it.'"

"You think he meant as a musician, an artist? You'll never have any success, you'll never be any good? That way?"

Matt shook his head. "I'm supposed to smuggle some coke into Paris tomorrow with Janice. She's done it a couple of times to make money: you put the coke in a condom, you swallow—"

"You're not going to do it, right? Right?"

Matt didn't answer.

Stevie put her hand on Matt's neck, her thumb gentle against his cheek. "You know what can happen?" she said. "You know how long it'll take that much coke to kill you? About two seconds."

Matt laid his head on her shoulder. "I'm out of money," he said. "I've been out of money for weeks. If I don't do this, I've got to go home."

Stevie was quiet for a time. She stroked Matt's hair, running her fingers over the back of his head and his neck. "I see my father sometimes in dreams," she said. "He was killed in the Falklands war, which no one even remembers anymore."

Matt tried to look up, but she was holding his head pressed tightly to her.

"I know it's not just a dream when we're standing under a big orange moon, because that really happened when I was very little. He held me on his shoulder under a moon just like that and told me always to remember it and the moment would never disappear. When we're standing under an orange moon like that, then he's visiting me and it's not just a dream."

"Do you believe that, really?" Matt pulled away from Stevie. "That the dead come back and talk to you?"

"Absolutely," she said. "You shouldn't go tomorrow. No matter what."

Matt turned over on his stomach and pressed his head into the mattress. "I told Janice I'd go with her," he mumbled. "She's expecting me to go with her." He felt sick. His stomach was jittery, on the edge of being nauseous.

Stevie lay her head on Matt's back. "What are you doing with that girl?" she asked, her voice not much above a whisper. "Do you even know what you're doing?"

Matt thought about Janice, about how he could explain her to Stevie. On the surface she looked like a brat. Her father was an earl or a duke, or some such title, and her family was wealthy—extravagantly wealthy. But she hadn't taken a cent from her family since she turned twelve. She had run away and been brought back time and again, until they just gave up on her. She had been making her own way for the last three years—mostly by smuggling drugs. She was fifteen. She had poems by Rimbaud committed to memory. She listened to Bartók and Frank Zappa. Matt had met her at a bar when he was still sleeping with Stevie and playing with the band. She had walked up to him and said, "Thirty-five thousand children die every day of starvation and my father has three homes." She was wrecked, of course. She was so high, she probably had no idea what she was saying. Matt had laughed and then felt stupid when Janice appeared hurt by his laughter. She had stumbled away before he could think of anything else to say.

Matt closed his eyes and fell asleep without realizing it. When he woke up, it was light out, and Stevie and the other woman were curled up together in a ball on the far side of the bed. The other woman was snoring lightly. He picked himself up slowly from the mattress, thinking he might have already made his decision, that Janice might already be in the air, on her way to Paris without him. He quietly left Stevie's room and entered the dark hallway. In the kitchen, he found Richie asleep on the floor, an ashtray full of roaches near his head and a gallon jug of wine held tightly to his chest, as if he were a child and the jug were a teddy bear. He looked around the room for a clock, but the walls were bare. The only furniture was a kitchen table, and the only thing on the table was Richie's guitar.

Matt stood quietly in the kitchen. He thought about what it would be like to call Cathy. She would be happy to get his call. She might not act that way at first, but she would be happy. When he left the apartment and went out to the street, he saw a husky old man unlocking the doors to a newspaper stand; and, behind the newspaper stand, a steady stream of people descending the stairs into the tube station. If he called Cathy, she'd book him a seat on a flight home. When he got off the plane, she'd be there at the airport, waiting. She'd tell his parents, and they'd be there, too, as well as her parents. It would be a party, a reunion, a welcome home: he could see Cathy standing there, picture her face, round like his own, her shoulder-length brown hair falling toward her shoulders, the ends turned under in a satiny curl. She was not an especially attractive girl, though she certainly wasn't ugly. Matt thought of her as plain, a not very attractive girl. He had known her since she was thirteen. At the airport, his mother would cry. She would cover her mouth with her hands. The men would hang back. Then would come the embraces, the hugs and tears, the pats on the back—and he'd be home.

Matt asked the time at the newspaper stand. It was a little after seven. He started for his apartment. The Paris flight left at eight-fifteen from Heathrow. First he walked and then he ran, and when he opened the door to his room, he found Janice standing by his bed, glaring at him. She pointed to his guitar case, which was in the middle of the floor. "I broke the lock," she said. "I thought you'd just split."

Matt closed the door by leaning against it. "I fell asleep," he said. "I woke up with a dream that—"

"There's a cab on the way," Janice said. "I'm all ready. If you want to do this thing with me . . ." She gestured toward the back of the chair where Matt's clothes were waiting.

In her navy blue skirt and white blouse, with her hair pulled back in a ponytail and her face scrubbed clean of makeup, Janice looked like a child, like a little girl. For a moment, Matt didn't move. He stood there as though he were paralyzed. Janice stared at him, waiting, and the look in her eyes was a question: What's it going to be, Matt? What are you going to do? Matt's hand moved slowly toward the buttons of his flannel shirt. He imagined again the airport scene as he arrived home: his parents and Cathy's, Cathy walking toward him.

Then he remembered a summer night when he was a senior in high school: both families had come to one of his baseball games to watch him play; he had his own cheering section in the bleachers. After the game, Cathy's two little brothers came running across the field to him, as if he were a hero. His parents went

home, and he went to Cathy's, where Cathy and her mother pre-
pared dinner while he drank a beer with her father and talked
about the game. After dinner they all watched television, and after
her parents went to bed, he made out with Cathy until they were
both half-naked and supremely frustrated, and then he went
home, where his mother had waited up for him and wanted to
know how the night had gone. The memory of that night felt like
a great weight, or like a pressure suit—something that enclosed
him and pressed against him. He undid the top button of his shirt
and looked again at Janice, who was looking back at him now with
curiosity, like a scientist observing the behavior of an animal.

"Matt," Janice said, her voice not angry. "Just tell me. Are you
coming with me or not?"

Matt nodded.

"You're coming?"

He nodded again.

Janice pushed his hands away and began undoing the buttons
of his shirt. "You're scared," she said. "I was scared the first time,
too. I was terrified." She leaned into him and peeled the shirt off
his back.

Matt wanted to tell her about the dream, but the words weren't
coming. When she unfastened his belt and pulled his jeans down
around his thighs, he sat on the bed and lifted his legs. She knelt
in front of him and let his feet rest in her lap while she untied his
shoelaces and pulled off his boots. Matt was watching Janice
undress him, but he was thinking about his uncle.

Once, when he was a boy of eight or nine, he had bicycled to
his uncle's farmhouse. He hadn't told his parents because this was
a period of time when the talk about his uncle was all hushed and
solemn. From hearing the grown-ups, he knew that his uncle
Mike had been to war in Vietnam. He had heard bits and pieces
of things about drugs and shootings. He had heard some things
about women. His uncle kept leaving town and coming back, as if
the town were a prison and he could never manage a successful
escape; and every time he came back, he looked stranger. He had
a beard. No one else in the family had a beard. He had long hair.
No one else in the whole town, that Matt knew, anyway, had long
hair. This time when Matt bicycled to the farmhouse, it was one

of the times when his uncle had just come back from being away, and everybody was whispering about him. Matt had bicycled the full ten miles out of town to the rundown farmhouse where his uncle lived, and he had found him asleep in his living room. He remembered that the house had been neat, but weirdly decorated: hubcaps were nailed to the wall in the kitchen and living room, and his uncle's sculptures that he made out of farm junk were displayed on tables and in nooks and crannies, places where anyone else in his family would have placed a lamp or a knickknack—and there was a closed-up wooden crate in the kitchen, hanging by a chain from the ceiling, the kind of crate that's made of wire and thin wood.

This one was closed, and a padlock was looped through the wire, so that you'd have to break the crate to open it. Inside the crate was a candle. It was round and it was big, the size of a carnival fishbowl. It was rust-red with a thick black wick that was lit and burning. Wax dripped down the sides of the candle and onto the crate and through the slats to the floor. Matt looked at the crate with the lit candle, and he couldn't imagine why anyone would do such a thing: put a lit candle inside a locked wooden crate. He tiptoed into the living room, where his uncle was sleeping in a tilted-back recliner with a bottle of whiskey on the floor beside him. He was wearing a crisp white T-shirt with I ♥ WISCONSIN printed beneath an idyllic picture of a farmhouse surrounded by barns and silos and cows lazily chewing grass in a pasture. He was curled up in the chair, hugging his chest, his arms underneath the T-shirt, as if it were a straitjacket. Matt remembered being struck by the contrast between that clean white T-shirt and his uncle's haggard face and jaundiced-looking skin and long, stringy, unwashed hair. He had never told his uncle about the visit, his uncle or anyone else.

This was the uncle who had come to him in his dream. This was the uncle who had told him he'd never make it.

When Janice finished undressing him, Matt stood up and put on the cordovan penny loafers and the khaki slacks, the blue shirt with the button-down collar and the London Fog overcoat. Janice brushed his hair for him and kissed him on the cheek. "Don't be scared," she whispered. "We can do it," she said, and she took him by the arm, gently, and had him sit on the floor by the bed and tilt his head back, the way he had seen her do it, and open his mouth wide.

First he closed his eyes; then he opened them and he watched her coat the outside of a condom with some kind of a gel before she lowered it into his mouth and began pushing it down his throat. He gagged the first time, and she told him to relax.

Outside, the cabbie honked his horn. Janice opened the window and yelled that they'd be right down. Then she came to him again, and this time he closed his eyes, and he imagined what they'd look like as they boarded the plane, like a brother and sister, like a couple of kids going off by themselves on a journey, and he relaxed and tried to ignore the pain as best he could, the feeling like he was being ripped open at the neck as she pushed the condom down his throat.

ABOUT GARY SOTO

A Profile by Don Lee

In one of his essays, Gary Soto writes that as a child, he had imagined he would "marry Mexican poor, work Mexican hours, and in the end die a Mexican death, broke and in despair." The statement might seem surprising, coming as it does from such a well-established writer. Considered one of the best Chicano poets of his time, Soto has published over twenty books, including seven volumes of poetry, the latest of which is *New and Selected Poems* (Chronicle Books). In addition to fellowships from the Guggenheim Foundation, the NEA, and the California Arts Council, he has received the American Book Award from the Before Columbus Foundation, the Andrew Carnegie Medal from the American Library Association, and the Levinson Award from *Poetry,* among numerous other honors.

But it is a desperate fate that anyone who grew up with Soto would have predicted for him as well. Recently, Soto attended his junior high school reunion, and he was disheartened to learn how many of his childhood friends had ended up in prison or been killed. Yet no one seemed particularly shocked by the news. His own outcome as an author and a senior lecturer in Berkeley's English department provoked more disbelief. "No, that's gotta be somebody else, man," his classmates said. "You must be copying this stuff out of a book, Gary."

Soto was born in 1952 in Fresno, California, the center of the San Joaquin Valley's agricultural industry, and everyone in his family was a field or factory worker. His father packed boxes at the Sunmaid Raisin Company, and his mother peeled potatoes at Redi-Spuds. Soto himself picked grapes and oranges, collected aluminum, hoed cotton and beets—anything he could do to help out. Red-lining was still legal then, and they were confined to Mexican-American neighborhoods. When Soto was five, his father was killed in an industrial accident. His mother eventually remarried and moved the family to a mostly Anglo area of Fresno,

PHOTO: CAROLYN SOTO

but nonetheless, Soto could never envision a future absent of borderline poverty and violence. "The likelihood of going beyond that was minuscule," he says.

In turn, not much was expected of Soto—a wild, mischievous kid who got into his share of trouble at school. "One of the aspirations was that if we stayed out of prison, we would be fine. As long as we did that, there was a reason to be proud." What might have saved him, just as he was flirting with real danger, was a school program called the Cadets, a military club. Through it, he learned some discipline, although it could hardly be said that the drills improved his academics. Indeed, he finished high school with a D average.

It was somewhat of a miracle, then, that he didn't flunk out of Fresno City College, where he enrolled in 1970 to avoid the draft. Initially, he chose to study geography. "I figured I'd just look at maps, study some rivers, take multiple-choice tests, and that'd be that. Being semi-illiterate, I didn't want to be forced to write anything." He was, after all, a *pocho*, a Mexican American who was neither here nor there, who didn't belong to either culture, whose Spanish and English were both poor, whose family did not and does not, to this day, read books—not even Soto's work, although they are the first to boast about his accomplishments.

Thus, it took enormous faith—and perhaps a little arrogance—for Soto to believe he could write poetry after being introduced to it by happenstance. At a library, he picked up an anthology, *The New American Poetry*, edited by Donald Allen. The poems—by Edward Field, Gregory Corso, Kenneth Koch, Allen Ginsberg, and Lawrence Ferlinghetti—were lively, irreverent, and audacious, and Soto was hooked. "I thought, Wow, wow, wow. I wanted to do this thing." He transferred to California State University, took workshops with Philip Levine, and fell in with a group that would eventually be known as the Fresno School of poets, which included Leonard Adame, Omar Salinas, Ernesto Trejo, and Jon Veinberg.

In 1974, Soto graduated magna cum laude from Cal State with a degree in English, then received his M.F.A. from the University of California, Irvine, in 1976. The next year, Soto's first book of poems, *The Elements of San Joaquin,* was published by the University of Pittsburgh Press. Critics praised the book—as well as the volumes that followed, *The Tale of Sunlight* and *Where Sparrows Work Hard*—for Soto's frank, desolate portrait of migrant life, his short, enjambed lines and idiomatic diction, and his ability to shift from naturalism to magic realism, from the apocalyptic to the transcendent.

However, the reception to his work was not completely free of reproach. One of the respected *veteranos* of Chicano literature now, Soto was occasionally admonished in the seventies for not overtly addressing the socio-economic aspects of Mexican-American life. The *movimiento*—the movement begun by Cesar Chávez when he organized California food harvesters into the United Farm Workers—was still raging in the San Joaquin Valley, and the Vietnam War, though winding down, was still extant, and Chicano artists were being pressured to adopt the zeitgeist of cultural nationalism and anti-establishment rhetoric. "There were a lot of people who couldn't quite understand what I was doing," Soto recalls. "They'd say, 'Hey, man, how come you're not talking about things that are political?' I was really groping at the time, and if I had gotten lost in that, I don't think I would have recovered." Instinctively, he knew that the more personal he was in his work, concentrating solely on his individual experiences, the more universality he could attain.

If anything, Soto turned more and more inward as the years went by. He published three books of essays—"narrative recollections," he called them—in the eighties: *Living Up the Street, Small Faces,* and *Lesser Evils.* Writing prose, he discovered a new freedom. "I felt I could be louder, more direct, also sloppier, whereas with poetry, I believed you had to control your statement, not be so obvious." The prose collections, which were almost strictly autobiographical, also presented something else that was different: a more mature, ironic, and humorous view of his childhood, finding celebrations of joy amid the hardships of growing up in the barrio.

Unexpectedly, he began receiving fan letters, one or two a week, from teenaged Mexican Americans, which convinced him to try writing for children and young adults. In 1990, he came out with *Baseball in April,* which won the Beatty Award and was recognized as the American Library Association's "Best Book for Young Adults." To date, 80,000 copies of *Baseball in April* have been sold. "I began to feel like I was doing something valuable," Soto says. "I thought I might be able to make readers and writers out of this group of kids." He has continued writing—in addition to his literary work—short stories, poems, and novels for young adults and picture books for children, and he has amassed an extraordinary audience for them, selling over half a million copies of his books. He has also produced three short films for Mexican-American kids.

Yet paradoxically, Soto can't quite shake the insecurity of being a *pocho* from Fresno. He follows a comfortable daily routine at his house in Berkeley, writing in the morning, tackling correspondence in the afternoon, then working out (he has a black belt in tae kwon do and is now studying aikido); in the evening, he spends time with his wife of twenty years, Carolyn, whom he met in college, and their daughter, Mariko. By all measures, Soto should feel assured about his place in the world, but he still doubts his ability to write, still fears that his latest poem will be his last good one—anxieties exemplified by a game he used to play with his wife:

"I would be working on a book of poems, and I'd say to her,

'Do you like this?' and she would nod her head. I would decide, more or less, which poems to save by how many nods she gave me. But I'd be so nervous, waiting for her reaction. I'd think, Oh my God, maybe I'm a fraud, maybe this woman's going to call the Bureau of Consumer Fraud on me. I have to keep reminding myself that after all these books over all these years, I must be doing something right."

BOOKSHELF

Recommended Books · Spring 1995

THE INVISIBLE CIRCUS *A novel by Jennifer Egan. Nan A. Talese/Doubleday, $22.50 cloth. Reviewed by Jesse Lee Kercheval.*

My copy of the *Harper's Book of Quotations* insists that Henry Ford really said, "History is *more or less* bunk," instead of the shorter, blunter version usually attributed to him. Either way, most Americans would probably agree. History is something you learn in school, something safely corralled in textbooks. History is not something that affects you personally. Contemporary American fiction tends to reflect this belief. If it deals with history, it is the history of an individual or, at most, a nuclear family. Recent history, the sixties and seventies, when it appears at all, tends to be the province of the Vietnam vet, as if only by making the mistake of going to war, of leaving the shores of America, do you run the risk of becoming part of a larger whole.

But in her marvelous first novel, *The Invisible Circus,* Jennifer Egan takes up the burden of history and shows clearly how those turbulent decades shaped the lives of her characters. The novel opens in 1978. Seven years before, Phoebe O'Connor's charismatic sister, Faith, a genuine San Francisco flower child, fell or jumped or was pushed off a cliff in Italy. The mystery of what happened to Faith plagues Phoebe, who is now eighteen and feels sealed off from the truth by a "white door," her present life "unreal and without significance": "What mattered was hidden from sight. At times she hated remembering, wanting nothing in the world but to rush forward into something of her own, lose herself in it. But this wasn't possible. The only way forward was through that door." With the help of Faith's postcards, Phoebe runs away to Europe, determined to recreate her sister's fatal journey.

On her trek across Europe, Phoebe finds the burned-out remnants of the once vibrant counterculture world. In Paris, she even takes a trip in the classic sixties sense, taking a hit of LSD in a scene that climaxes in her hurling herself at a plate glass window, behind which she thinks she sees her sister, literally throwing herself at the past. In Berlin, she meets up with Wolf, her sister's old boyfriend and traveling companion, and together they set out for Italy to find the truth behind her sister's death.

Along the way, we learn about Phoebe's family in the days before her father's death from cancer and Faith's presumed suicide. In some of the strongest writing in the book, the father, a failed painter, encourages Faith's reckless behavior time and time again as a way of making up for a life spent working at IBM. It becomes clear that after his death, Faith could only keep going, wild to wilder, until she found herself standing on that cliff overlooking the sea. When Phoebe is finally able to locate and visit the cliff, she is "riven, then, by a vision of her sister unlike any she'd had before: a girl like herself, reaching desperately for something she couldn't see but sensed was there, a thing that always seemed to evade her."

Only rarely does Egan's deft touch at integrating history into her characters' lives fail. The Baader-Meinhof gang, for instance, reads a bit too much like archival footage. But for every occasional weak spot, there are a dozen luminous evocations of the period. To read *The Invisible Circus* is to see the sixties again in all its glimmering and illusive promise.

Jesse Lee Kercheval's novel, The Museum of Happiness, *was published by Faber and Faber last year. She is finishing a new novel,* Paulo and Claudia, *based on her story "Brazil," which appeared in* Ploughshares.

RAIN *A novel by Kirsty Gunn. Grove/Atlantic, $15.00 cloth. Reviewed by Jessica Dineen.*

In New Zealander Kirsty Gunn's first novel, *Rain,* twelve-year-old Janey and her five-year-old brother, Jim, fight the loss of their innocence as their parents' world encroaches upon them. They live by an enormous lake, where they play alone, seduced by the solace and mystery of the water, while their parents fill the house with adults each night for raucous parties. Only occasionally do Janey and Jim pass through the drunken adult world, their mother's earrings "jangling" and bracelets "clicking," ice "clinking" in the glasses. Their parents and guests view the children as objects of entertainment, jostling and frightening the small, delicate Jim, whom they all want to touch, as Janey is trapped by the lewd attention of men. Always, the children escape to the dark lakeside, where they "glide into the shallows like eels, the silky black water parting, closing behind us without a sound. On into the deep we swim, out to where the lake is lapping into endless night."

The ebb and flow of Gunn's prose, her unabashedly sensuous and precise description, draws the reader into Janey's perceptions as she narrates the story. For her, the passage of time—the seasonal swelling of the lake, darkening of the sky, deepening of the water as the children swim offshore—is both terrifying and inviting. After all, she does love her spent, hungover parents, and feels an inevitable pull toward that adulthood of bright lipstick and swishing dresses. But she is bound by the need to protect Jim, and in doing so, she hopes to preserve herself, stave off adolescence: "The lovely bend of his fine limbs was the dream I had for my own body, to be light and careless and ... in endless, continuous motion of flight."

Rain is not without flaws. At times the theme of impending change seems forced, and the story—less that one hundred pages long, more a novella than a novel—is too thinly told in places, but Gunn's haunting book is redeemed by its sheer grace. Janey's fear of seeing the depth of her parents' failures is poignant and ironic, for their true failure has been in wasting their lives, becoming a shallow, "dried out" remnant, merely "what was left," of a promising past.

The book ends tragically, and the sad impossibility of real escape for the children is no surprise—traces of doom are present throughout the story. Gunn concludes *Rain* with language from a manual on life-saving techniques, and while the effect seems artsy at first, the passage very skillfully affords the reader with a sudden objectivity. The tragedy is turned before us like one of the mother's jewels, and the loss seems more terrible for its clarity, the story more compelling.

WILD RIDE *Essays by Bia Lowe. HarperCollins, $20.00 cloth. Reviewed by Bonnie Friedman.*

Bia Lowe's lovely first book, *Wild Ride,* uniquely combines nature essays with personal narrative. Each piece—composed of succulent, sweet prose—is a thought pagoda, ideas storied one atop another, from sneezes to alfalfa to sexual betrayal to Halley's comet to urban animals to an image of her newlywed parents conceiving her: "Their cells mingle hundreds of times before a fluke will yank me from the Void."

Lowe uses one association to focus another, one intensely observed phenomenon to grind the lens of another. Her theme is the most ancient—asking how the body relates to the spirit. Lowe writes: "Sometimes when I visualize my interior, I see something like an inverted night sky, a galactic depth where vain spirits wail and rhapsodize. . . . Yet the world laid open by the surgeon's scalpel is pure gore, an arrangement of wet, blood-colored sacs . . . our hearts . . . sing to be outside the Earth's time, where bodies blaze steadily like stars."

In fact, darkness haunts these essays, which crystallize, rock-candy style, around the themes of bats, blood, skunk smell, horror movies, the underworld, and that constant stalker, death. Lowe uses darkness to pool light, ink to catch constellations. She recounts being visited one midnight by "light in the form of a gingerbread figure. Someone without features, fingers or genitals, just radiance the color of magma."

Magma. In *Webster's,* magma is defined as "molten rock material within the earth from which an igneous rock results by cooling." It's easy to see why Lowe is attracted to the word. Here is her obsession with fire-made-flesh, the sparkling shudder congealed into the opaque body.

One essay chimes through the next in this book, much as one section of an essay—depicting dance class, say, or a cave journey—rings inside another, similar to the way some story collections are cast as novels. This book is the nonfiction equivalent. It adds up. It comes to more than the accumulation of itself. Within the greenhouse of each essay, orchids bloom, glories are forced—by the sheer hot intensity of the author's attention—to display themselves. Despite the Paganini prose, despite the jeroboams of description, one never senses emotional idleness.

Lowe truly writes as if her life depends on it. Riff by riff she descends to the spooky, cat-strewn, anxious, resinous, shadowy core, and lets her eye be a camera.

"Night is rapture for bats," and for her, too. "Songs are cast like nets, to ensnare dazzling nightscapes." Bia Lowe's sentences try to do the same thing, and succeed.

Bonnie Friedman is the author of Writing Past Dark: Envy, Fear, Distraction, and Other Dilemmas in the Writer's Life *(HarperCollins).*

GHOST LETTERS *Poems by Richard McCann. Alice James Books, $9.95 paper. Reviewed by Rafael Campo.*

A dear patient of mine, a poet himself, who died not too long ago from complications of AIDS, once explained to me why he spent so much of his precious time and energy writing. "My poems are in a sense the physical impression of me that I will leave behind in this world, almost like a ghost," he said. In this forceful first collection of poems by Richard McCann, whose eery title, *Ghost Letters,* establishes a communication between this realm and the netherworld, the dead are indeed restored to their physical bodies—never to haunt us, but rather to awaken us to the possibilities of reconciliation, healing, and desire in our own lives.

In what medium other than poetry as attentive and sensuous as McCann's could such an elusive correspondence be conducted? "There's no moon now. / Its sharp arc's fallen. How can I tell where it was? / *If I could reach into the darkness,* you said— / Or if I could reach beyond the exhalation of my breath..." he writes at the end of the long poem "Feast of Salt," pinpointing precisely the intimate space in the imagination where these dialogues are allowed to happen. What transpires in this work is never merely a figment of the imagination, however; even the most obstinate of skeptics will find ample documentation of the physical evidence. Eschewing filmy apparitions, showy special effects, and cobwebbed memories, these poems are full of the harsh breath, the warm flesh, and the jutting bones of their subjects: "What I could not accept was how much space / his body was taking with it," he writes of rubbing his emaciated lover's back in the opening poem, "Nights of 1990": "*So this / is the spine,* I thought, this articulation / of vertebral tumors, this rope of bulbous knots; / *tissue,* I thought, as I studied his yellowing skin— / tissue, like something that could tear." One wishes only for more of the iambs and rhymes of the physical processes McCann otherwise so carefully records.

Many of the most satisfying poems in this collection, which received both the 1994 Beatrice Hawley Award and the 1993 Capricorn Poetry Award, thus confront with an unflinching eye the devastation wrought by AIDS. At once mournful and intensely erotic, full of astonishment at the steadfastly witnessed collision of sexual desire with undeniable mortality, the poems create a portal for the passing of souls; to stand in the circle of their music is to perform along with them a kind of blessing and valediction. The poem "After You Died" creates rich harmonies as it sings in these differently pitched themes: "I had a body. And I could recall / how it had been, back then, / to want things. Easy to recall that now— / this sun-dazed room; lilacs in white bowls. / But for a long time I was grateful / only for what your dying was taking from me."

The reader, in turn, is grateful for what McCann takes from the world, and what—through the same alchemical process—he returns to it; burned away is all the bitterness, and in its place the reader discovers the unexpected softness and delicacy of ashes. Since these poems are ghost letters, in truth they can never be so destroyed, even as they consume themselves in their blazing energy. Richard McCann has written a moving missive to all of us, one which relates its terrible news with quiet grace, great conviction, and, in the end, inextinguishable pleasure.

Rafael Campo is completing his medical residency at the University of California, San Francisco. His first book of poems, The Other Man Was Me, *was published by Arte Público last year, and a collection of his essays is due out from W.W. Norton this autumn.*

A MURIEL RUKEYSER READER *Poems and prose by Muriel Rukeyser, edited by Jan Heller Levi. W.W. Norton & Co., $25.00 cloth. Reviewed by M. L. Rosenthal.*

It is a delight to see Muriel Rukeyser in print again. Her intimately self-searching lyricism and her identification with the world's insulted and injured have a special place in our poetry. As were the poet-prophets Whitman, Crane, Lawrence, and her deeply admired Hugh MacDiarmid, Rukeyser, too, was a driven artistic experimenter.

Like them, she could hazard sheer rhetoric, not always happily but often reaching heights of beautiful intensity. Her forays into impassioned poetic reportage—in *U.S. 1* (1938), for example, about the ravages of silicosis among West Virginia coal miners—are strikingly effective. And throughout her writings, her penetrating intellectual force is a vital factor. Thus, her first volume of poems, *Theory of Flight* (1935), reflects her study of aeronautics, implicitly relating it to her own efforts to learn to fly a plane and also to her youthful familial and psychological travails. And her most ambitious prose work, *Willard Gibbs* (1942), brilliantly connects the literary and scientific awakening and the political fires of mid-nineteenth-century America.

Her work had begun as part of the wide-open poetic scene of the twenties and thirties. But after World War II, that atmosphere, with its formal explorations and its testing of revolutionary and bohemian lines of thought, began to dissipate in the odd period of self-repression that lasted until the Beats came along. Always able to publish her books, Rukeyser was nevertheless at a disadvantage in the burgeoning McCarthy period. Despite early praise by John Crowe Ransom and Kenneth Burke (and my own later discussions of her work, many of which are collected in *Our Life in Poetry: Selected Essays and Reviews*, as well as in other critical books), she was slighted or ignored critically for a long time.

Rukeyser was one of our country's most politically committed yet undoctrinaire poets. Her courage was seen in her journey to Spain during the Civil War and in the serious part she played in the Ban-the-Bomb movement, the resistance to the Vietnam War, and the struggles for civil rights and women's rights. Equally courageous was her endurance of the trials of single motherhood before the great shift in attitudes toward such matters had taken place.

All this is reflected in the sensitive, chronologically arranged selections by Jan Heller Levi of Rukeyser's poems and prose writings—including excerpts from *Willard Gibbs* and the wise, intensely personal *The Life of Poetry* (1949). But the charm and wit of, say, a poem like "From the Duck Pond to the Carousel" tells us as much about the mind behind it as does its author's graver writing. The ambivalences, the conflicting pressures, and the comic and ironic turns in her work are characteristic of the species *poeta germanus*.

Rukeyser was, indeed, a true poet. It is impressive to go back to her sequence "The Book of the Dead" in *U.S. 1* and see her handling of the Congressional investigation of Union Carbide and Carbon for its indifference to the deadly lung disease afflicting its miners. The mixture of modes (descriptive passages, documentary materials and testimony, and lyrical choruses) makes for a memorable achievement in poetic dynamics. But the same volume also contains unforgettable individual lyrical pieces—among them "Homage to Literature," which begins: "When you imagine trumpet-faced musicians / blowing again inimitable jazz"; and "Nuns in the Wind," with its desperate clowning: "All that year, the classical declaration of war was lacking. / There was a lot of lechery and disorder. / And I am queen on that island."

Muriel Rukeyser can be happily compared with such international figures as MacDiarmid, Auden, and Neruda. Theirs is a poetry that grows out of the rich modern history of the art and is inextricably enmeshed in the political and cultural struggles—or agonies—of its own age.

M. L. Rosenthal's most recent book of poetry is As for Love: Poems and Translations *(Oxford University Press). His most recent critical book is* Running to Paradise: Yeats's Poetic Art *(Oxford).*

THE STONECUTTER'S HAND *Poems by Richard Tillinghast. David R. Godine, $19.95 cloth. Reviewed by Diann Blakely Shoaf.*
Eleven years after the publication of *Our Flag Was Still There*, Richard Tillinghast has assembled a fourth full-length collection, *The Stonecutter's Hand*, that solidifies and deepens the considerable achievements of his earlier work. Tillinghast's new volume of poems will be followed in a few months by his critical book on Robert Lowell, and while many of the best poems in *The Stonecutter's Hand* show the influence of Tillinghast's former teacher, that influence has been masterfully assimilated.

In the book's first eight poems, the reader is shuttled between locales as various as Turkey, Belgrade, and Dublin. The contemporary travel poem has received a great deal of well-deserved opprobrium in recent years, but Tillinghast escapes any personal and cultural solipsism—a major risk of the genre—through a historical sense that operates on both emotional and intellectual planes, and through a Bishopian gift for self-effacement. "Impedimenta of the self / Left behind somewhere," begins Tillinghast in the volume's opener, "Anatolian Journey"; his speaker's luggage consists only of those items that will facilitate his immersion in an alien realm, such as "a bag with good straps, a book of Turkish proverbs, / Sandals of proven leather, / A bottle of water called, yes, 'Life' / In the language of the country." But Tillinghast would slough off even further impedimenta, move beyond the language of the country to the language of the earth, which knows neither checkpoints nor border crossings: "in the morning wake to / Acres of sunflowers / warmer than any human welcome; / Haystacks domed like the domes of whitewashed mosques, / And the Black Sea rising out of itself / like the fragrance of remoteness."

As the volume's use of traditional form makes clear, Tillinghast's technical facility has matured into virtuosity. Of particular interest are his stanzaic poems which represent variations on the six-line "Venus and Adonis" stanza, rime royal, ottava rima, and Spenserian stanza. Tillinghast displays in "Abbey Hill" and "Passage," to mention only two, an earned canniness as regards the melding of form with content. What form could better suit a recounting of the pulling down of an Anglo-Irish great house than rime royal, its very name seeming brutally ironic in the context of the poem's subject matter? And what better than ottava rima to recall another of Tillinghast's tutelary spirits, Yeats, who is paid homage in several poems, among them the piece from which *The Stonecutter's Hand* carves its title? Tillinghast's most stellar accomplishment in form, however, is perhaps an unconscious one. In poem after poem modeled on the historical English stanzas, he changes the pattern of lines which would conventionally follow an *abab* pattern to *abba,* and the formal allusion to the "In Memoriam" stanza splendidly but subtly emphasizes the elegiac undercurrents of *The Stonecutter's Hand.*

The Irish are notorious sentimentalists, and after a year spent in Galway, it's probably to Tillinghast's credit that his emotional rein goes slack only a time or two in this new collection. Yeats's insistence on packing the rawest of feelings in ice and salt is probably an influence here, as well as the muscular exactitude of language for which Lowell is justly famous, especially in those triple adjectives: "flabby, bald, lobomotized" is transformed by Tillinghast's native music to a phrase like "toppling, armorial, hierarchic." Yet sentimentality can also take the form of cynicism, and while Tillinghast is mercilessly self-confronting and self-questioning in the journey represented by *The Stonecutter's Hand,* his final stance is one of a Heaneyesque attention to the world's numinousness. But an attention purely American, purely Tillinghast's own.

Diann Blakely Shoaf is a frequent reviewer for the "Bookshelf." Her collection of poems, Hurricane Walk, *was published by BOA Editions in 1992.*

EDITORS' SHELF *Books recommended by our advisory editors.* **Andre Dubus** recommends *If the Tiger,* a novel by Terry Farish (Steerforth): "Ms. Farish has written a taut, fast-paced novel about the young daughter of a pilot in the Gulf War and a young woman who is a Cambodian refugee. In New Hampshire and Lowell, Massachusetts, the young women are in flight from the Cambodian husband and on a quest for family love. I love this beautiful, short book, and I want to read it again." **Don Lee** recommends *Living to Be 100,* stories by Robert Boswell (HarperPerennial): "A richly imaginative, truly wonderful collection of short stories. Where other writers would stop, Boswell always goes one unexpected, delightful step further." **Philip Levine** recommends *What We Carry,* poems by Dorianne Laux (BOA Editions): "Gritty, tough, lyrical poems that depict the actual nature of life in the West today." **Gail Mazur** recommends *Open Water,* a novel by Maria Flook (Pantheon): "Maria Flook's people in *Open Water* are the product of her full-hearted embrace of an American kind of nuttiness and a zest for their strange self-induced troubles. The margin, which is their habitat, is wildly, deliciously drawn by a writer of enormous intelligence and insight into our character." **Joyce Peseroff** recommends *Germany,* poems by Caroline Finkelstein (Carnegie Mellon): "When a Jewish woman chooses *Germany* as the title for her book of poems, she is telling you something about language and history. Caroline Finkelstein writes with radiance about an implacable world where '. . . the yews move, / . . . the ragged cedars flutter, and the Tigris and the Rappahannock flow.' In her lexicon, the portrait of a dying child succored by Mama and Papa (one of several based on Roman Vishniac's photographs of Warsaw) is 'sentimental,' since the girl's fate is transport, madness, and death in a concentration camp. These poems are arrows to the heart, sharp with the knowledge of human impulse and fletched with the beauty of human language." **Robert Pinsky** recommends *Each in a Place Apart,* poems by James McMichael (Univ. of Chicago): "An extraordinary book-length poem or sequence about love and failed love; absolutely original formally, yet clear and plain." **Christopher Tilghman** recommends *Safe in America,* a novel by Marcie Hershman (HarperCollins): "Marcie Hershman has interwoven a family saga with the triple threats of the Holocaust, war, and AIDS. She presents these calamities as family tragedies, revealed in the heartbreaking ordinariness of daily life. Her story, with its ironic title, should make everyone consider his or her blessings while recognizing the vulnerabilities that are now native to us all." **Chase Twichell** recommends *Blood Thirsty Savages,* poems by Adrian C. Louis (Time Being): "Louis writes rough, smart, honest poems that cut through all the polite twinges of political correctness. Tenderness is one side of the blade, and rage the other. His Native America is not the one we normally hear about, stripped as it is of the usual generic references. Instead it's human passion, savvy, and grief that light up the world, which we recognize as our own."

EDITORS' CORNER *New books by our advisory editors.* **Russell Banks:** *Rule of the Bone* (HarperCollins, May 1995), a novel about a homeless, drug-addicted teenager living on the edge of society. **Gail Mazur:** *The Common* (Univ. of Chicago), her third collection of poems, of which Lloyd Schwartz comments: " 'Dislocated' in Houston, New Englander Gail Mazur writes that she's determined to look at her new surroundings 'with the wise tough eye of exile.' She succeeds—partly because, like so many of our very best poets, she is everywhere in exile; and within this darkness, she turns the flashlight of her tough, ironic wisdom on both herself (her fear, her ambition, her courage, her foolishness) and the common 'animal' life around her (family, students, friends—animals, too), then, beaming even farther outward, on the larger world's daily games (baseball, politics, war). Knowing, cheeky (*'Is that it, Gail,/the wish you make in your happiness?'*), palpably sensuous ('yellows//like sulphur, like lemons, like fresh butter,/ not golden, or blazing, but homely—'), and painfully close to home—these poems and what they achieve are anything but common." **Sue Miller:** *The Distinguished Guest* (HarperCollins), a novel about a couple who must care for the husband's mother, an acclaimed author— a situation that forces them all to reconcile with the past. **Gerald Stern:** *Odd Mercy* (W.W. Norton, July 1995), a new book of poetry, including a 56-page poem called "Hot Dog" about a street woman in New York's East Village.

POSTSCRIPTS

Miscellaneous Notes · Spring 1995

CONTRIBUTOR SPOTLIGHT Tim Seibles is a commanding, dynamic presence, particularly when he reads his poetry. Tall, charismatic, he stands behind the podium and gives animated voice to poems that are, at turns, grave, inventive, and hilarious. His primary subjects from the start have been sexuality and race, and somehow, Seibles has always been able to *engage,* not alienate, people when he addresses these delicate topics—an attitude he wishes could be adopted by society overall.

The author of two full-length collections, *Body Moves* and *Hurdy-Gurdy,* and a just-released chapbook, *Kerosene,* Seibles was born in Philadelphia in 1955. His mother was a high school English teacher, his father a biochemist for the Department of Agriculture. As a child in Germantown, Seibles loved to read, especially books on Greek and Roman mythology. He wanted to write science fiction novels, yet his obsession was to become a professional football player. He chose to attend Southern Methodist University in Dallas because his idol, Jerry Levias, one of the first black college players of prominence, had gone there. Seibles had not played organized football until his senior year in high school, but he was athletically gifted enough to make the SMU team as a freshman walk-on. To his chagrin, however, a new coach immediately instituted a wishbone offense, focusing on the running game, and Seibles, a wide receiver, hardly stepped onto the field.

He quit in his sophomore year, just as poet Michael Ryan was starting a creative writing program at the university. Seibles, always willing to try anything, took his workshop, then more workshops with Jack Myers and John Skoyles, and before he knew it, he had discovered a new passion. He read James Dickey, Mark Strand, Ai, Morton Marcus, Pablo Neruda, Margaret Walker, Leroi Jones, W. S. Merwin, and countless others, and he loved them all—"the rhythms, the radical visions, the sense that there was a place for deep, unbridled feelings," Seibles says.

After graduating, he substitute-taught English and worked as a stereo salesman, writing poems on the side. He had no plan for his life, really, and he certainly didn't think he'd stay in Texas, but he drifted into teaching English full time, first at inner-city North Dallas High School for eight years, then at the Episcopal School of Dallas for another two. Though he found the innocence of most teenagers compelling, he was frustrated that many of them had already become apathetic and cynical about education.

Seibles, on the other hand, remained relatively naive, particularly about his poetry. "Being young," he says, "you just don't know that you're outnumbered." He kept writing and sending out poems, undeterred by the "millions of rejections," then enrolled in the low-residency M.F.A. program at Vermont College in 1987. Under the tutelage of Mark Cox, Jack Myers again, Richard Jackson, and Susan Mitchell, he developed a fondness for longer, sprawling poems, captivated by "how tension and momentum are sustained in a narrative." In 1988, Corona Press published his first book,  *Body Moves,* and shortly afterwards, he retired from teaching high school, cashing in his pension, and rushed headlong into the poet's life. He received fellowships from the NEA and the Fine Arts Work Center in Provincetown (where he became the Writing Coordinator), won the Open Voice Award for poetry from the National Writers' Voice Project at New York's West Side YMCA, and published his book, *Hurdy-Gurdy,* with Cleveland State University Press. For the last year, he has been living in Cambridge, and in the fall, he will teaching creative writing and literature at the college level.

The poem "Ten Miles an Hour," on page eighty-eight of this issue, is a telling example of Seibles's abiding concerns. He began the poem sitting in Logan Airport in Boston, musing about the speed of light, watching passengers of multiple races and nationalities milling about the airport. Nine months later, when the poem started taking shape, he almost put it away. "It seemed too giddy and weird at first. I thought people would say I was oversexed." But he liked the hip, homeboy voice, its rhythm and pop, and decided, "The roof is coming off, you just have to take it to the bridge."

Seibles explains further: "I was, and still am, interested in how we, as people and artists, can cultivate hope for a future that isn't simply a prolongation of nightmare. There's a real sense that the world isn't working, that it's become this bloody, ugly, consumptive, diseased, fearful place that's unlivable. I'm interested in asking how we might see beyond this without putting guns to our heads. 'Ten Miles an Hour' became an emblem of mad hope—for a wilder, freer, sweeter world with all these different people of different races, with the erotic realm representing a utopian locus of pleasure and possibility and connection."

Kerosene, his new chapbook from Ampersand Press, is an extension of this meditation on race, and he uses various personas for expression, including Malcolm X and Quai Chang Caine, the character on TV's *Kung Fu*. "The book," Seibles says, "moves between the polarities of delight and rage. Largely, it's about the sense of alienation that accompanies being non-white in this country." He does not support violent revolution, nor does he subscribe to any separatist ideologies, which he thinks are "short-sighted and cowardly," but he warns that we are nearing a threshold, beyond which the only response to racism and its persistence *can* be rage. "If you're black, there's a growing feeling that things are being squeezed around you, as if your body is taking up too much space in America. There's a kind of power wielded by people of privilege, mainly whites, that they're completely unaware of. It's as if you're in a room with a giant. You're so small, the giant doesn't realize you're there. He throws his arm around, knocks you to the ground, and he doesn't even notice. And maybe he won't until you burn the house down."

Seibles loathes the idea of reaching that level of impasse. Ultimately, he wants to promote reconciliation by asking us, as a nation, to reconsider the dynamics of power between whites and non-whites. "For society to work, we're going to have to take a hard look at what assumptions people who are white Americans can make that people who aren't cannot make, and how that damages our connection to one another. We don't want to spend the rest of our lives angry, do we?"

In the meantime, he'll keep two photographs in his wallet—one of Martin Luther King, Jr., one of Jimi Hendrix—that he has carried since his days at SMU. They helped form Seibles's credo in college, which, he admits, might sound corny and idealistic and quaint, but is more relevant today than ever: "Love, peace, unity, harmony, brotherhood."

Kerosene is available for $7.00 postpaid from Ampersand Press, Box 642, Creative Writing Program, Roger Williams University, Bristol, RI 02809. Copies may also be obtained through the Grolier Poetry Book Shop's mail-order service in Harvard Square by calling (800) 234-POEM.

TUFTS AWARDS Thomas Lux, one of our advisory editors, won the third annual Kingsley Tufts Poetry Award for his book *Split Horizon* (Houghton Mifflin). The $50,000 award from the Claremont Graduate School is the largest poetry prize given for a single work. Doug Anderson, whose work was included in the "Emerging Writers" issue edited by Marie Howe and Christopher Tilghman (Winter 1992–93), was also honored by the Claremont Graduate School. He was the recipient of the second annual $5,000 Kate Tufts Discovery Award for Poetry for his book, *The Moon Reflected Fire* (Alice James Books).

NPS Since 1978, the National Poetry Series has sponsored the annual publication of five books of poetry, selected by a rotation of distinguished judges. The winners for 1994 are: Erin Belieu for *Infanta* (Copper Canyon), chosen by Hayden Carruth; Pam Rehm for *To Give It Up* (Sun and Moon), chosen by Barbara Guest; Matthew Rohrer for *A Hummock in the Malookas* (W.W. Norton), chosen by Mary Oliver; Samn Stockwell for *Theatre of the Animals* (Univ. of Illinois), chosen by Louise Glück; and Elizabeth Willis for *The Human Abstract* (Viking Penguin), chosen by Ann Lauterbach.

PHONE-A-POEM HIATUS We are temporarily discontinuing Phone-a-Poem. We will announce the status of its resumption in a future issue. Many thanks to Joyce Peseroff, who was no less than heroic in maintaining the service for the past four years as a volunteer.

CONTRIBUTORS' NOTES

Ploughshares · Spring 1995

NIN ANDREWS is the author of *The Book of Orgasms*. Her work has appeared in *The Paris Review, Michigan Quarterly Review, Denver Quarterly,* and many other reviews. THOMAS BELLER was born and raised in New York City, where he now lives. His stories have appeared in *The New Yorker, The Southwest Review, Epoch, Mademoiselle,* and *Best American Short Stories 1992*. His collection of stories, *Seduction Theory,* will be published by W.W. Norton in May 1995. He is one of the founding editors of the art/literary magazine *Open City*. RON BLOCK is the author of *Dismal River: A Narrative Poem* (New Rivers). His poem "Strip Joint" is part of a longer narrative sequence entitled *Poems from the Twilight Drive-in*. MICHELLE BOISSEAU's *No Private Life* was published by Vanderbilt University Press in 1990. Recent poems have appeared in *The Gettysburg Review, The Southern Review, Crazyhorse, Green Mountains Review, The Journal,* and *Cream City Review*. An NEA fellow in 1989, she is currently an associate professor of English at Morehead State University in Kentucky. DANIEL BOURNE's first book of poetry, *The Household Gods,* will appear this year from Cleveland State University. His work has been in *Field, The American Poetry Review,* and elsewhere. He spent 1985-87 in Poland on a Fulbright to work with Polish writers, for whom his translations appear widely. He teaches at the College of Wooster, where he edits *Artful Dodge*. BECKY BYRKIT recently published her first book of poems, *Zealand,* which was nominated for the Western States' Book Award by SUN/Gemini Press. Her first published poem appeared in *Ploughshares* after her house burned down in 1987, and somewhat less flammable material has appeared since then in *New England Review, Exquisite Corpse,* and *Best American Poetry 1994*. She recently completed her second book, *BirdDog Real,* and lives on the Greek island of Corfu. MARCUS CAFAGÑA's poems have been published or are forthcoming in *Poetry, Agni, Seneca Review, The Iowa Review, The Kenyon Review,* and *Harvard Review*. His book manuscript, *The Broken World,* was chosen as a semi-finalist in the 1995 Brittingham Prize in Poetry. CATHLEEN CALBERT has recently published poems in *The Paris Review* and *Feminist Studies,* and her work is forthcoming in *The Hudson Review, Poetry Northwest,* and *TriQuarterly*. She is an assistant professor at Rhode Island College. THOMAS CENTOLELLA recently received a Lannan Literary Award. His first book, *Terra Firma,* was selected by Denise Levertov for the National Poetry Series. His next book, *Lights and Mysteries,* is due from Copper Canyon Press this fall. He lives in San Francisco and teaches in the Bay Area. NICOLE COOLEY is a recipient of a 1994 "Discovery"/*The Nation* Award. She received her M.F.A. from the Iowa Writers' Workshop, and her poems have appeared in *Poetry, Field, The Nation, Poetry Northwest, Willow Springs,* and other magazines. ROBIN COOPER-STONE

lives in Norfolk, Virginia, and is currently applying to graduate writing pro-
grams. Her poetry recently appeared in *Another Chicago Magazine*. SUSAN
DODD is the author of four books of fiction, most recently *Mamaw* and *Hell-
Bent and Their Cities.* She currently teaches in the graduate writing program at
Bennington College and has recently completed a new story collection, *O Care-
less Love.* She lives in Ocracoke, North Carolina. MARTÍN ESPADA is the author
of five poetry collections, most recently *City of Coughing and Dead Radiators*
and the forthcoming *Imagine the Angels of Break,* both from W.W. Norton. His
awards include two NEA fellowships, the PEN/Revson Fellowship, and the Pat-
terson Poetry Prize. Espada teaches in the English department at the University
of Massachusetts–Amherst. EDWARD FALCO has published stories recently in
The Atlantic Monthly, The Southern Review, and *TriQuarterly.* He is the author
of a collection of stories, *Plato at Scratch Daniel's & Other Stories* (Arkansas,
1990), and a novel, *Winter in Florida* (Soho, 1990). He teaches fiction writing at
Virginia Tech. RICHARD GARCIA is the author of *The Flying Garcias* (Pitts-
burgh, 1993). He has earned fellowships and grants in poetry from the NEA and
the California Arts Council, and he received the 1993 Cohen Award from
Ploughshares for best poem. He is currently the poet-in-residence at Children's
Hospital, Los Angeles. DAGOBERTO GILB is the author of the novel *The Last
Known Residence of Mickey Acuña* (Grove). His collection of stories, *The Magic
of Blood* (Grove), was a finalist for the PEN/Faulkner Award and won the
PEN/Hemingway Foundation Award. ELIZABETH GRAVER's short story collec-
tion, *Have You Seen Me?* (Ecco, 1993), was awarded the 1991 Drue Heinz Litera-
ture Prize. Her stories have appeared in *Prize Stories 1994: The O. Henry Awards*
and *Best American Short Stories 1991,* and in such journals as *Story, Antaeus, The
Southern Review,* and *The Southwest Review.* She teaches English at Boston Col-
lege and has recently completed a novel. CORRINNE HALES's most recent book
of poems is *Underground* (Ahsahta), and her poems have appeared recently or
are forthcoming in *Prairie Schooner, The North American Review, The Massachu-
setts Review, Poetry East, Quarterly West,* and elsewhere. She teaches creative
writing at California State University, Fresno. JANA HARRIS has published five
books of poetry, including *Oh How Can I Keep On Singing?: Voices of Pioneer
Women* (Ontario), and one novel. She teaches creative writing at the University
of Washington and lives on a farm in the foothills of the Cascade Mountains,
where she raises horses. BOB HICOK is an automotive die designer. The 1995
recipient of the University of Wisconsin's Felix Pollak Prize for his collection
The Legend of Light, he has new poems due out in *Chelsea, Indiana Review, Poet-
ry, Quarterly West,* and *The Southern Review.* PETER MARCUS has published his
work in *Poetry, New England Review, Agni, The North American Review, The
Iowa Review,* and *Ploughshares,* and his poems are forthcoming in *Prairie
Schooner* and *The Quarterly.* He recently completed his first manuscript of
poems, *Dark Remedies.* Presently, he is a post-doctoral fellow in psychology at
Boston College. DELOSS MCGRAW's paintings have been exhibited and collected
throughout the United States and Europe. He is a literary artist and has collabo-
rated with numerous authors—most often with the poet W. D. Snodgrass.

Recently, he illustrated his third children's book with author Edward Lear, *The New Vestments* (Simon and Schuster). His work is currently available through the Mary Ryan Gallery in New York City. In 1997–99, the Scottsdale Museum of Contemporary Art will tour a major exhibition of McGraw's paintings, sculptures, and book art from coast to coast. McGraw lives in the Phoenix and San Diego areas. The cover painting is in the collection of Barton and Bea Thurber of San Diego. JACK MYERS's latest volume of poetry is *Blindsided* (Godine, 1993), and he is the author of eleven other volumes of or about poetry. He has won awards from the NEA and the Texas Institute of Letters, among others, and teaches creative writing at Southern Methodist University and in the Vermont College M.F.A. Program. LEONARD NATHAN's latest books are *Carrying On: New and Selected Poems* and, with Arthur Quinn, *The Poet's Work: An Introduction to Czeslaw Milosz*. He is now finishing a new volume of poems and a book on bird-watching. He is a professor emeritus of the University of California, Berkeley. NONA NIMNICHT, who lives in Oakland, California, has published poetry and reviews in a number of magazines, most recently in *Poetry Northwest, Quarterly West,* and *The South Florida Poetry Review.* CORNELIA NIXON's novel-in-stories, *Now You See It,* was published by Little, Brown in 1991 and HarperCollins in 1992. A story of hers will appear as the first-prize winner in *Prize Stories 1995: The O. Henry Awards.* She is also the author of a book on D. H. Lawrence. SUZANNE PAOLA has a book of poems, *Glass,* out in the *Quarterly Review of Literature*'s Poetry Series, published in January 1995. She has poems appearing in *The Yale Review, The Partisan Review,* and other journals. V. PENELOPE PELIZZON grew up in Boston. She has an M.F.A. from the University of California, Irvine, and is now a Ph.D candidate at the University of Missouri, where she is writing a series of essays on May Swenson and a collection of poems. JOSEPHINE REDLIN grew up on a small farm in South Dakota. In 1994, she finished her M.A. in creative writing at Fresno State, where she was the recipient of the 1992 Ernesto Trejo Prize and a 1993 AWP Intro Award. Her poems have recently been published in *The Antioch Review, The Journal, New England Review,* and *North Dakota Quarterly.* KENNETH ROSEN has published several chapbooks with Ascensius Press of Portland, Maine, the latest of which is *Reptile Mind.* His poems in this issue will appear in his forthcoming collection *No Snake, No Paradise.* DIXIE SALAZAR currently teaches writing at California State University, Fresno, and the Corcoran State Prison. She has published in numerous magazines, and has a chapbook, *Hotel Fresno,* and a novel, *Limbo,* forthcoming this spring. MAUREEN SEATON was a 1994 recipient of an NEA fellowship and an Illinois Arts Council grant. Her books are *The Sea Among the Cupboards* (New Rivers, 1992) and *Fear of Subways* (Eighth Mountain, 1991). She has recent poems in *The Kenyon Review* (edited by Marilyn Hacker), *The Paris Review, New England Review,* and elsewhere. TIM SEIBLES is the author of three books of poetry, *Body Moves* (Corona, 1988), *Hurdy-Gurdy* (Cleveland State, 1992), and *Kerosene* (Ampersand, 1995). An NEA fellow in 1990, he recently received the Open Voice Award from the National Writers Voice Project. See page 204 for a profile on Seibles. REGINALD SHEPHERD's first collection of poetry, *Some Are Drowning,* which won the 1993 AWP Award in Poetry, is available from University of Pittsburgh Press. The poems in this issue are from his second collection, entitled *Angel, Interrupted,* which will be published by Pittsburgh in the fall of 1996. MARK SVENVOLD, recent recipient of a grant from the Ludwig Vogelstein Foundation, has published his work in *The Atlantic Monthly, Under 35: The New Generation of American Poets,* and *The Virginia Quarterly Review.* He lives in New York City. JON VEINBERG lives and works in Fresno, California. A 1993 recipient of an NEA fellowship, he is the author of *An Owl's Landscape* (Vanderbilt University).

∼

SUBMISSION POLICIES *Ploughshares* is published three times a year: usually mixed issues of poetry and fiction in the Winter and Spring and a fiction issue in the Fall, with each guest-edited by a different writer. We welcome unsolicited manuscripts from August 1 to March 31 (postmark dates). All submissions sent from April to July are returned unread. In the past, guest editors often announced specific themes for issues, but we have recently revised our editorial policies and no longer restrict submissions to thematic topics. If you believe your work is in keeping with our general standards of literary quality and value, submit it at anytime during our reading period. If a manuscript is not suitable or timely for one issue, it will be considered for another. Please send only one prose piece and/or up to five poems at a time (mail prose and poetry separately). Poems should be individually typed either single- or double-spaced on one side of the page. Prose should be typed double-spaced on one side and be no longer than thirty pages. Although we look primarily for short stories, we will, very occasionally, publish personal essays and memoirs. Novel excerpts are acceptable if they are self-contained. Unsolicited book reviews and criticism are never considered. Please do not send multiple submissions of the same genre, and do not send another manuscript until you hear about the first. Additional submissions will be returned unread. Mail your manuscript in a page-sized manila envelope, your full name and address written on the outside, to the "Fiction Editor," "Poetry Editor," or "Nonfiction Editor." (Unsolicited work sent directly to a guest editor's home or office will be discarded.) All manuscripts and correspondence regarding submissions should be accompanied by a self-addressed, stamped envelope (S.A.S.E.) for a response. Expect three to five months for a decision. Do not query us until five months have passed, and if you do, please write to us, including an S.A.S.E. and indicating the postmark date of submission, instead of calling. Simultaneous submissions are amenable as long as they are indicated as such and we are notified immediately upon acceptance elsewhere. We cannot accommodate revisions, changes of return address, or forgotten S.A.S.E.'s after the fact. We do not reprint previously published work. Translations are welcome if permission has been granted. We cannot be responsible for delay, loss, or damage. Payment is upon publication: $10/printed page for prose, $20/page for poetry, $40 minimum per title, $200 maximum per author, with two copies of the issue and a one-year subscription.

the Common

GAIL MAZUR

"**Generous, thoughtful, moral without being moralistic**, the poems become that shared, public space in which we recognize the intersections of disparate histories and the singular nature of the everyday: *The Common*."—Alice Fulton

"Gail Mazur writes in *The Common* about the 'inexhaustible reality' of her life in America, touching 'things about to vanish.' **Her masterful poems are both sad and witty**—is there better praise?"—Adam Zagajewski

"In her new book of poems, *The Common*, Gail Mazur continues to tell the passionate truth about herself and life in beautifully made poems. They are **the work of a mature, deeply engaged, and productive artist**."—Alan Dugan

Paper $11.95 88 pages

Phoenix Poets series

THE UNIVERSITY OF CHICAGO PRESS
5801 South Ellis Avenue, Chicago, Illinois 60637

**BENNINGTON
SUMMER
WRITING
WORKSHOPS**

July 2-July 15 &
July 16-July 29,
1995

■

2-week or 4-week residencies in

Fiction, Nonfiction, Poetry

ACADEMIC CREDIT
AVAILABLE

For more information, contact:
Priscilla Hodgkins, Assistant Director
Bennington Summer Writing Workshops
Bennington College, Box S
Bennington, Vermont 05201
802-442-5401, ext. 160
Fax: 802-442-6164

FACULTY:

Barbara Lazear Ascher
Elizabeth Cox
C. Michael Curtis
Stephen Dunn
Lynn Freed
Rebecca T. Godwin
Lucy Grealy
Linda Gregg
Ann Hood

Carole Maso
Alice Mattison
Askold Melnyczuk
Cecile Pineda-
Leneman
Debra Spark
Gerald Stern
Bruce Weigl

READERS:

David Broza
Jamaica Kincaid
Nuyorican Poets
Liam Rector

Stephen Sandy
Jordan Smith
Anne Winters

EDITORS & LITERARY FOLK:

Judith Doyle
D.W. Fenza
Elizabeth Gaffney
Forrest Gander
Nan Graham
Elizabeth Grossman
Fiona McCrae

Sheila Murphy
Shannon Ravenel
Irene Skolnik
Peter Stitt
Alexander Taylor
Christina Ward
C.D. Wright

MFA

Writing Program
at Vermont College

Intensive 11-Day Residencies

July and January on the beautiful Vermont campus, catered by the
New England Culinary Institute. Workshops, classes, readings, conferences,
followed by **Non-Resident 6-Month Writing Projects** in
poetry and fiction individually designed during residency.
In-depth criticism of manuscripts. Sustained dialogue with faculty.

Post-Graduate Writing Semester

for those who have already finished a graduate degree
with a concentration in creative writing.

Vermont College admits students
regardless of race, creed, sex or ethnic origin.

Scholarships and financial aid available.

Poetry Faculty

Robin Behn	Jack Myers
Mark Cox	William Olsen
Deborah Digges	David Rivard
Nancy Eimers	Mary Ruefle
Juan Felipe Herrera	Betsy Sholl
Jonathan Holden	Leslie Ullman
Richard Jackson	Roger Weingarten
Sydney Lea	David Wojahn

Fiction Faculty

Carol Anshaw	Ellen Lesser
Tony Ardizzone	Brett Lott
Phyllis Barber	Sena Jeter Naslund
Francois Camoin	Christopher Noel
Abby Frucht	Pamela Painter
Douglas Glover	Sharon Sheehe Stark
Diane Lefer	Gladys Swan
W.D. Wetherell	

For More Information

Roger Weingarten, MFA Writing Program, Box 889,
Vermont College of Norwich University, Montpelier, VT 05602
802–828–8840

Low-residency B.A. & M.A. programs also available.

The Nobel Laureates of Literature

SAUL BELLOW
JOSEPH BRODSKY
CAMILO JOSÉ CELA
ODYSSEAS ELÝTIS
NADINE GORDIMER
HALLDÓR LAXNESS
GABRIEL GARCÍA MÁRQUEZ
NAGUIB MAHFOUZ
CZESŁAW MIŁOSZ
TONI MORRISON
KENZABURO ŌE
OCTAVIO PAZ
CLAUDE SIMON
ALEKSANDR SOLZHENITSYN
WOLE SOYINKA
DEREK WALCOTT

A Special issue of

The Georgia Review
Spring 1995

PRESENTED BY

 THE ATLANTA COMMITTEE
FOR THE OLYMPIC GAMES
CULTURAL OLYMPIAD

IN COLLABORATION WITH
The Georgia Review

As part of the Nobel convocation on 23-25 April 1995,
the Spring 1995 issue will contain original critical essays
on the sixteen living laureates, reprints of the Nobel citations,
their Stockholm lectures, and photographs of each laureate.
To reserve your copy of this special issue
(scheduled for publication on 15 March 1995),
please remit $8.00 for a single copy, or $18.00 for a one-year
(four issues) subscription (to begin with the Spring number) to:

The Georgia Rewiew
The University of Georgia, Athens, GA 30602-9009
or call **1-800-542-3481**

PITTSBURGH
Poetry Series

Photo: Leonard L. Greif, Jr.

Red Under the Skin
Natasha Sajé
Winner of the 1993
Agnes Lynch Starrett Poetry Prize
"Intelligence flashes, winks, gleams and dances every-where in this book, along with human compassion, full and precise sensuousness, an acknowledgment of appetite, and a knowledge of history."—Alicia Ostriker
$10.95 paper

Photo: Austin Chick

Some Are Drowning
Reginald Shepherd
Winner of the 1993 Associated Writing Programs'
Award Series in Poetry
Selected by Carolyn Forché
This first collection of poems enacts the struggle of a young black gay man in his search for identity. Many voices haunt these poems: black and white, male and female, the oppressor's voice as well as the oppressed. The poet's aim, finally, is to rescue some portion of the drowned and the drowning. *$10.95 paper*

Photo: Margaret Wallace

Time's Fancy
Ronald Wallace
"Wallace has an inventive and witty imagination which takes him into all sorts of surprising directions. His work is not only sure in its craftsmanship, but humanly impor-tant in its subject matter and treatment. Best of all, it is exuberantly alive."—Lisel Mueller.
"His poems ring with validity."—Richard Hugo
$10.95 paper

Available at local bookstores, or

UNIVERSITY OF PITTSBURGH PRESS
c/o CUP Services, Box 6525, Ithaca, NY 14851   800-666-2211

The Madison Review

A literary magazine published semiannually by the University of Wisconsin
Department of English

announces its

PHYLLIS SMART YOUNG POETRY PRIZE

&

CHRIS O'MALLEY FICTION PRIZE

WINNERS OF THE YOUNG AND O'MALLEY PRIZES
RECIEVE $500 AND PUBLICATION IN THE MADISON REVIEW.
ALL ENTRIES MUST BE RECEIVED IN THE MONTH OF SEPTEMBER.
SEND ONE STORY OR THREE POEMS
(POEMS SHOULD BE UNDER FOUR PAGES EACH).
MANUSCRIPTS WILL NOT BE RETURNED.
ENTRY FEE IS $3.00 PAYABLE TO THE MADISON REVIEW.
INCLUDE SASE WITH ALL CORRESPONDENCES AND SUBMISSIONS.

YOUNG/O'MALLEY PRIZES
c/o THE MADISON REVIEW
UNIVERSITY OF WISCONSIN-MADISON
DEPARTMENT OF ENGLISH
MADISON, WI   53706